The Second Coming

Dawn of the Millennium

Kirk Nelson

Wright Publishing Company • Virginia Beach, VA

Temple photo courtesy of the *Biblical Archaeology Review* (April-March 1983 issue).
300 Connecticut Ave.
Washington, DC 20008

ISBN 0-961 7119-0-6

Table of Contents

VI

To Sandra

Foreward

This book is about the most important event in human history, the Second Coming of Jesus. All of us realize that we are presently in a period of unparalleled economic, political, and social change, and it is the belief of many that the culmination of this upheaval will be the Second Coming and the beginning of the Millennium. Proof of this will be presented in this book, and I hope it will convince those who are skeptical that the time is not far off.

One of the main purposes of this book is to link two different types of Second Coming prophecies, namely, the fundamentalist prophecies and the New Age prophecies. Most people are familiar with the fundamentalist view of prophecy from Hal Lindsey's best-selling book, *The Late Great Planet Earth* (which sold over 15,000,000 copies). The most renowned New Age prophet is the Virginia Beach psychic, Edgar Cayce, made famous by Jess Stearn in his best-selling book *Edgar Cayce, the Sleeping Prophet.* I believe there is a pattern of agreement in these two types of prophecy, and it will be my endeavor to prove this.

Since the fundamentalist prophecies are based on literal interpretation of the Bible, the Bible passages we will examine will in large part be interpreted from that point of view. Some of these interpretations will be familiar to Bible students because they are explained in many books by Bible scholars. Fundamentalists lean toward literal interpretations, and New Age people lean toward symbolic interpretations, but it is my belief that both methods are essentially in agreement on the basic points.

We will look at Bible chapters and verses that prophesy the Second Coming of Jesus. We will give specific attention to the "Olivet Discourse" in which Jesus speaks to His disciples about His return. Since Jesus refers to the Book of Daniel, we will see what predictions Daniel made.

We will examine the readings of Edgar Cayce, probably the most famous psychic in American history.

To give added weight to our hypothesis of when the Second Coming will occur, we will review predictions from Nostradamus, the Great Pyramid, the Dead Sea Scrolls and the Hopi Indians.

After we find out what is prophesied, the timetable of events, and when the Second Coming is likely to occur, we will learn what we, individually and collectively, can do to prepare ourselves for His return.

Lest we take any predictions too seriously we should remember the case of William Miller whose story is retold in the following quote from the book *Did Jesus Write This Book?* by Charles Francis Potter.

"The nineteenth and twentieth centuries have also produced prophecies of the 'end of days.' The last century brought the once-famed William Miller, an American who founded a sect named after himself. Like his predecessors of the A.D. 999 hoax, Miller calculated his end-all date from biblical mathematics, particularly those obscure calculations in Daniel (8:14). Christ will return on March 21, 1843, or March 21, 1844, Miller told his followers, who prepared their ascension robes in readiness for their translation into heaven. Twice the faithful gathered for the glorious meeting, and twice nothing happened. 'The World is reeling to and fro like a drunkard,' the leader assured the Millerites, but all that appeared in the sky were ominous rings around the sun, and the awesome tail of the great comet of 1843, measuring 108,000,000 miles in length."

"Sorrowfully, after this double fiasco, the only world to end was Miller's. Thousands of followers deserted him. A broken man, he died alone in his Vermont home, discredited and beaten by his own honest delusion."

Unlike the Millerites, we should not don our ascension robes and prepare for the end. But there are certain signs which will tell us when the Second Coming is close. These signs are, I believe, clearly discernable and will become apparent to many people as the time draws near.

"Coming events cast their shadow before"
                    —Goethe

The End of the Age

How do we know that we are nearing the time of the Second Coming? The Bible provides us with signals to look for as evidence of the "end of the age." The first of these is mentioned in Daniel 12:4. It states:

4   But thou, O Daniel, shut up the words and seal the book, even to the time of the end; many shall run to and fro, and knowledge shall be increased.

This passage tells us that at the time of the end, transportation and knowledge will be greatly increased. The increase in transportation has come largely in the last hundred years with the invention of the automobile and the airplane. The automobile has become as much a part of us as our legs, and airplane travel has become commonplace. The Civil Aeronautics Board estimates that in 1974 airplanes in the United States alone carried 207 million passengers over 162 billion passenger miles. This is an incredible amount of travel for one nation, and the world statistics are even more astronomical.

The increase in man's knowledge in all areas has been well documented, one of the most dramatic illustrations being the landing of men on the moon. Dreamed of as a fantasy at one time, it is now past history. The growth in college enrollment also reflects the growth in knowledge. Colleges which once had enrollments of 4,000 now have enrollments of 20,000 or more. A full 60% of high school graduates in this country go on to college, and the learning they receive there is more extensive than it has been in the past.

New discoveries in the field of science have accelerated faster than our learning institutions can teach. Physicists have broken matter into smaller and smaller particles, and astronomy has taken us to the farthest reaches of visible light. Some well known scholars have suggested that our society is in a state of cultural shock because of the explosive increase in information, but as we know, this is only the beginning.

Therefore, I feel that the two aformentioned criteria of increased knowledge and transportation have definitely been met within the last century.

Let's look at some key events Jesus cites in the Bible as preceding His Coming:

Matthew 24: 3-14:
3   And as He sat upon the Mount of Olives, the disciples came unto Him privately saying. Tell us, when shall these things be? And what shall be the sign of thy coming, and the end of the age?
4   And Jesus answered them and said unto them, Take heed that no man deceive you.
5   For many shall come in My name, saying, I am Christ; and shall deceive many.
6   And ye shall hear of wars and rumors of wars; see that ye be not troubled; for all these things must come to pass, but the end is not yet.
7   For nation shall rise against nation, and kingdom against kingdom; and there shall be famines, and pestilences, and earthquakes, in various places.
8   All these things are the beginning of sorrows.
9   Then shall they deliver you up to be afflicted, and shall kill you; and ye shall be hated of all nations for my name's sake.
10 And then shall many be offended, and shall betray one another.

11 And many false prophets shall rise, and shall deceive many.

12 And because iniquity shall abound, the love of many shall grow cold.

13 But he that shall endure unto the end, the same shall be saved.

14 And this gospel of the kingdom shall be preached in all the world for a witness unto all nations; and then shall the end come.

As mentioned in verse 14, one of the keys to the end times will be that Christianity will have been preached in all the world, to all nations. This requirement was not fulfilled completely until this century, when the Western World finally reached out to all the countries with whom little contact had previously been made. Christian missionaries and influences have now traveled to every nation in the world. China, Russia, Japan, India, and the continents of Africa and South America — all have experienced substantial exposure to the tenets of Christianity. As Jesus said, a "witness unto all nations" has indeed been the case.

Jesus also tells us that earthquakes, famines and pestilence will be seen in the period before the Second Coming. The increase in world population and the interdependency of countries on each other for food makes the world particularly vulnerable to famine. Many populous countries like India, for instance, have to import grain from the United States just to feed their own people.

Wars often can be the cause of intense famine, since fighting interrupts the normal flow of commerce. In Southeast Asia after the United States pulled out of Vietnam, Vietnam invaded Cambodia causing starvation among the war's refugees. Relief efforts were organized by several countries, but were hampered by a lack of cooperation on the part of the Vietnamese.

In the Horn of Africa war and famine have accompanied one another in the conflict between Somalia and Ethopia. Lack of rain plus the war have dealt a double blow to the people of that region, and many thousands have died of starvation.

It is true that we have always had problems in the world with famine, but toward the end of the age these problems will be intensified. Scientists are concerned about a growing trend among underdeveloped countries to overgraze semiarid or desert land, allowing the topsoil to be blown or washed away. This process is known as desertification. The fear is that more and more of the world's useable land is being lost in this manner, thus increasing the world food problem. And in this case, the countries being hurt are the countries that can least afford it.

One possible food production problem we have in this country is the loss of farmland to highways and suburban development. Thousands of acres are lost in the United States each year in this manner. Some experts predict that by the 1990s the United States will not be able to feed itself. Hopefully, increased yields per acre and intensified farming efforts will prevent this from happening.

Those who are aware of the prophecies concerning famine have organized companies to sell freeze-dried foods for storage during lean times. These "survivalists" have started a booming business out of the fears people have about the food supply. Most of the people involved keep up to a year's worth of food just in case the worst possible situation develops, and this is probably not a bad idea given the prophecy of Matthew 24.

Webster's New World College Dictionary defines pestilence as "any virulent or fatal contagious or infectious disease, especially one of epidemic proportions." With the increase in world travel, the possibility for the spread of infectious disease is greater than ever. Milder diseases such as the flu already spread quickly from nation to nation. Also, scientists now have the ability to produce hybrid bacteria by changing the DNA molecules in the cells themselves. The potential for the production of a "super germ" through recombinant DNA research has been the subject of court cases in several United States cities. It is a frightening possibility that such a germ could spread either by research accident or by a deliberate act of aggression from a hostile government. It could be months before scientists could identify such a germ, and find a method to fight it. While the United States has halted its germ warfare research, other countries such as the Soviet Union have continued to push forward their development programs.

An increase in the number of earthquakes is cited in Verse 7 as another clue to the beginning of the latter times. There have certainly been a number of earthquakes in the last few years. Algeria, Nicaragua, Italy, China, Indonesia and Iran have all been jolted by quakes. The eruption of Mt. St. Helens devastated a 100-mile area of Washington State and demonstrated graphically the intensification of geophysical activity. Such activity should grow as we approach the end of the century. Man has contributed to the increase by exploding nuclear weapons underground and by drilling deeper and deeper for oil. An underground nuclear test creates a mild earthquake which rates about 6.0 on the Richter scale. Hopefully, this testing will stop, but at present it continues.

During the past 30 years, deaths due to earthquakes around the world have increased from 13,000 in the '50s, to 300,000 in the '70s. And as we near the end of the age, we can expect to see even more severe earthquake activity.

Many authors have written about the possibility of earthquakes along the San Andreas fault in California. These prophets of doom have caused concern among people living along the fault especially around San Francisco and Los Angeles. While many earthquake predictions have not come true in the past, few scientists believe that these areas are safe from a major quake. Any increase in earthquake activity worldwide will affect the West Coast more than any other area in the United States and all the geophysical scientists know this.

Another Second Coming prerequisite is the rise of false Christs and false prophets. This can be seen in the increase in the numerous religious cults in the United States and around the world. These cults ask people to dedicate their lives to a "religious" leader and, more importantly, to give most of their money and possessions to him. The Rev. Jim Jones is the most tragic example in recent memory. His followers were so fanatical that over 800 killed themselves on his command. Other cults ask their members to spend their time raising money on the streets through any method short of stealing. Cult members often reject their families and friends completely to live the life of the cult. Anguished parents have resorted to hiring "deprogrammers" to help return some followers to normal life. It seems that many have already been deceived by false Christs and false prophets just as Jesus predicted.

Further on in Chapter 24 of Matthew is a statement that I believe definitely puts the Second Coming in the near future. It is verse 22:

22　And except those days should be shortened, there should be no flesh saved; but for the elect's sake those days shall be shortened.

As late as the early 1960s it was not within man's capacity to destroy all the flesh on the earth. But now, both the Soviet Union and the United States have more nuclear weapons with much greater megatonnage than the weapons of the early '60s. In fact, in the arsenals of the United States and Soviet Union are 50,000 tactical and strategic nuclear weapons. Further escalation of the arms race and technical advancements should make this firepower even more staggering. The unleashing of that much power and radio-activity within the relatively short period of time a nuclear war would entail would certainly destroy all life on earth. So it is obvious that things are not going to get so out of hand that the United States and the Soviets are going to exchange missiles in wholesale quantity. More likely, it will be the smaller nuclear powers who will be using atomic weapons. If the United States and the Soviets do use nuclear weapons, they will be of the tactical rather than the strategic variety, reducing the destruction to the battlefield alone.

As the Bible states, "if this time is not shortened" then man will destroy himself. It will be shortened, however, by a fantastic series of events, the first of which has already occurred.

Many writers in the 20th century have said that the country of Israel is the fulfillment of biblical prophecy. There is no doubt that this is so. The Jews are indeed the "chosen people" now, as they were 2,000 years ago when Jesus was born a Jew. During the time of the end, many of the world's events will revolve around the land of Israel. The return of the Jews to Palestine was predicted in the book of Ezekiel 34:13:

13   And I (God) will bring them (Jewish people) out from the peoples, and gather them from the countries, and will bring them to their own land, and feed them upon the mountains of Israel by the rivers and in all the inhabited places of the country.

This prophecy was fulfilled with the creation of the Jewish State of Israel in 1948. Since then, the Middle East has increased greatly in strategic importance because of the dependence of the Western world on Arab oil, and Israel is right in the middle of this vital region.

It seems incredible that the rise of Israel could have been predicted over 2,000 years ago by the Old Testament prophets. They foresaw the stubborn determination which would hold the Jewish people together throughout 1900 years of dispersement and move them to return to their own land in this century.

Any of the previously mentioned Second Coming prerequisites taken alone would not be very conclusive evidence, but all of them taken together makes for a convincing case, particularly when we realize that many of these were not fulfilled until the 20th century. Some did not occur until the last twenty years! Only very recently could it be said that most of the prerequisites for the Second Coming had already been fulfilled.

Since we obviously are close to the end time, the question arises: How soon will it be? Jesus gives us an idea in Matthew 24: 32-33:

32 Now learn a parable of the fig tree: When its branch is yet tender, and putteth forth leaves, ye know that summer is near.

33 So likewise ye, when ye shall see all these things, know that it is near, even at the doors.

Jesus tells us in this passage that when we see all these events the time will be very close. World affairs do seem to be headed toward a final culmination. However, there is one event preceding the Second Coming that is more important than all the others. It is called the Abomination of Desolation.

The Abomination of Desolation

Matthew 24:15-22

15 When ye, therefore, shall see the abomination of desolation, spoken of by Daniel the prophet, stand in the holy place (whosoever readeth, let him understand).

16 Then let them who are in Judea flee into the mountains;

17 Let him who is on the housetop not come down to take anything out of his house;

18 Neither let him who is in the field return back to take his clothes.

19 And woe unto those who are with child, and to those who nurse children in those days!

20 But pray that your flight be not in the winter, neither on the sabbath day;

21 For then shall be great tribulation, such as was not since the beginning of the world to this time, no nor ever shall be.

22 And except those days should be shortened, there should no flesh be saved; but for the elect's sake those days shall be shortened.

What is the abomination of desolation? It is a term that refers to the desecration of the Jewish temple in Jerusalem. This desecration occurs when a sinful object or thing is brought into the sacred part of the temple, where only the priests are allowed to enter. An example would be if a pig were offered on the holy altar, or if an altar to a pagan god were built in the holy place. A Syrian king, Antiochus Epiphanes, defiled the temple in just such a manner in 165 B.C. In order for another abomination of desolation to occur, the Jews must build a new temple.

The last Jewish temple in Jerusalem was destroyed in 70 A.D. by the invading Romans. However, since the Jews recaptured Jerusalem in the 1967 war, they have begun excavating the ancient temple site. There is one major problem though, and that is that the Moslem holy place, the Dome of the Rock, is built on the site of the old Jewish temple. So the temple mount is sacred to both the Moslems and the Jews. Just how important the temple site is to the Jews can be seen from this description of the Israelis' capture of the temple mount in 1967 after 2,000 years of dispersement:

> "The Israeli paratroop commander Mordechae Gur from atop Mount Olives ordered the final assault on the temple mount, "For two thousand years our people have prayed for this moment. Let us go forward."
>
> "Colonel Gur could not wait. He raced his halftrack down the mountain at top speed, hurling past the burned-out hulks of tanks and the sprawling bodies of slain paratroopers, then dodged by a flaming truck partly blocking St. Stephen's Gate and burst right into the Old City. White flags were beginning to appear on all sides. While his paratroopers reared in behind him, the colonel turned left, crashed through another gate and then sent back his message to GHQ: "The Temple Mount is ours. Repeat: The Temple Mount is ours." And despite the crackle of continued sniper fire, the first paratroopers rushed to the Western Wall, touched and kissed the sacred stones, then burst into tears at their triumph."[1]

[1] *Time Magazine,* April 12, 1982, p.30, New York, NY, "City of Protest and Prayer." Otto Friedrich.

The Western Wall is a holy place to the Jews because it is the outside wall of the temple that was destroyed in 70 A.D. Recently they have begun to excavate the area near it and the steps that led to the temple on the other side of the mount along the Southern Wall. Over the years layer after layer of debris has built up on the site of the old temple, and it will take some time to uncover it, but the work has begun.

In the Book of Exodus in the Old Testament are instructions for the construction of the temple and also instructions in how to perform the temple worship. Part of this worship involves the sacrificing of animals. This sacrifice is so important to the Jews that when they recaptured the temple in 1967, they wanted to begin again this daily ritual. The reason they did not is that they did not know the location of the old altar, as it is buried beneath the site of the Dome of the Rock.

The exact location of the temple's altar is important because according to Jewish law the sacrifice can only take place on the exact spot of the original altar. For many years it has been theorized that the altar was located under the Moslem holy place, the Dome of the Rock, from where, according to legend, Mohammed ascended into heaven. If the altar is beneath the Dome of the Rock, something will have to happen to the Moslem temple in order for the Jewish temple to be rebuilt there. This has been envisioned by some as a natural destruction by earthquake or man-made destruction by fire.

Religious zealots in Israel have already begun a campaign to rebuild the temple. Geula Cohen, a member of the Israeli Parliament, plans to introduce legislation that would open the temple mount to Jewish worshipers. Groups such as the Faithful of the Temple Mount (based in Israel) and the Jewish Temple Foundation (based in Denver, Colorado) are also calling for the "Third Temple" to be built. This movement has gone so far in Israel that a Jewish college in Jerusalem has begun training students in the rites prescribed for the priests in the Temple!

Since no plan exists in the Bible for building the temple,

this Third Temple movement might seem like a lot of sound and fury signifying nothing. But recently Israel's chief archeologist Yigael Yadin translated and published a 2,000 year old sacred writing called the Temple Scroll. In this scroll is an exact blueprint for the building of the temple including the dimensions of the courts and the location of all the temple's inner furnishings. It is amazing that this "blueprint" should come to light at the exact moment in history that the Jews have control over Jerusalem and are planning to rebuild the temple.

In recent years some archeologists have come to believe that the Jewish temple and the altar site are actually located farther north than the Dome of the Rock.[2] Attention has shifted to a small dome covering exposed bedrock on the northern edge of the temple platform. It is known as the Dome of the Tablets and is now believed to be the spot where the inner sanctuary, the holy of holies, was located. If it is proved to be the location of the holy of holies, then the temple can be rebuilt without disturbing the Moslem temple. This would remove a considerable obstacle to the building process, since disturbing the Dome of the Rock would cause a great outcry among the Moslems.

Jesus tells us that the abomination of desolation will "stand in the holy place." This is a very specific reference to part of the temple. The inner sanctuary of the temple has two parts: the holy place, and the holy of holies. Only the priests in their daily ritual are allowed to enter the holy place. It is the spot where they burn incense and light the lampstand. The holy of holies is the most sacred part of the temple which only the high priest is allowed to enter once a year on the Day of Atonement. On that day, the high priest enters the holy of holies and sprinkles the blood of the sacrifice on the mercy seat to make atonement for the sins of the Jewish people. The abomination of desolation, however, will not occur in the innermost sanctuary, but in the holy place just outside.

---

[2] *Biblical Archaeology Review*, March/April 1983, "Where the Ancient Temple of Jerusalem Stood," Asher S. Kaufman.

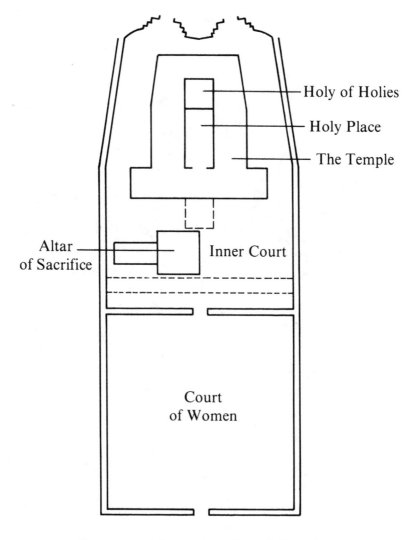

Holy of Holies

Holy Place

The Temple

Inner Court

Altar
of Sacrifice

Court
of Women

Diagram of the ancient Jewish Temple

In the foreground is the Dome of the Tablets where the Holy of Holies was located. In the background is the Dome of the Rock.

The fact that the abomination of desolation will occur "in the holy place" clearly shows that the temple must once again be rebuilt. This has happened before in history after the temple was destroyed by the Babylonians. At that time, the Jews were allowed to return to Jerusalem by Cyrus the Great, a Persian king, and rebuild the walls of the city and the temple.

When the temple is rebuilt again in a few years, we will see before us the physical symbol of Jesus' return to the earth. This is truly an exciting thought. The swiftness with which the Jews excavate the temple mount, rebuild the temple, and reinstate the daily sacrifice will give us clues as to the timing of events before Jesus' return.

There is a negative side to all this, however. Verses 16-22 mention a "tribulation," or, as it is usually referred to, the "great tribulation." This is a period of time which will be more tumultuous than any time that ever has been, or ever will be on the earth. It will begin immediately after the abomination of desolation. It will happen so suddenly, that people in Judea will not even have time to go into the house from the fields to get their clothes (Matthew 24).

The word translated "tribulation" here literally means "pressure" or "affliction." The great tribulation will be dominated by war, since the Jews would not permit their temple to be desecrated except by force. Any war involving the State of Israel would certainly involve the rest of the world including the United States. With the powerful weapons now possessed by more and more countries, the potential for this to be a very destructive war is great.

Since Jesus mentioned earthquakes and famine in the Olivet discourse, it seems that the great tribulation will have its share of these. The increasing world population and the interdependency of the world food supply make the possibility of famine fairly obvious. Combine this with the disruption of transportation and distribution facilities by war and earthquakes, and one could see how things could get very rough.

Many people believe that the great tribulation will cause

an allout nuclear war, however, verse 22 in Matthew 24 shows that this will not be the case. This is the "if these days were not shortened, then there would be no flesh saved" verse mentioned earlier. If tactical or theater nuclear weapons were used this would cause great suffering throughout the world, but it would not kill everyone as an allout nuclear holocaust would.

The abomination of desolation and the great tribulation are the two most important events preceding the Second Coming. Just what the timing of these events will be is made more clear by examining the parts of the Book of Daniel that deal with the abomination of desolation. The most important verses in this regard are:

Daniel 9:24-27

24 Seventy weeks are determined upon thy people and upon thy holy city, to finish the transgression, and to make an end of sins, and to make reconciliation for iniquity, and to bring in everlasting righteousness, and to seal up the vision and prophecy, and to anoint the most Holy.

25 Know, therefore, and understand, that from the going forth of the commandment to restore and build Jerusalem unto the Messiah, the Prince, shall be seven weeks, and threescore and two weeks; the street shall be built again, and the wall, even in troublous times.

26 And after threescore and two weeks shall the Messiah be cut off, but not for Himself; and the people of the prince that shall come shall destroy the city and the sanctuary, and the end of it shall be with a flood, and unto the end of the war desolations are determined.

27 And he shall confirm the covenant with many for one week; and in the midst of the week he shall cause the sacrifice and the oblation to cease, and for the overspreading of abominations he shall make it desolate, even until the consummation, and that determined shall be poured upon the desolate.

This vision was told to Daniel by the angel Gabriel. Gabriel was also the messenger who foretold the birth of Jesus to Mary. Only a message of supreme importance would come from this high a source.

The "seventy weeks" referred to in verse 24 are prophetic weeks in which each "day" represents one year. The word translated "week" actually means "seven" and therefore it refers to 7 years, the cycle of the Jewish Sabbatical year, and not to a 7-day week. Thus, the seventy "weeks" actually equals 490 years. These years run chronologically, but not continuously. In other words there is sometimes a break in the occurrence of these years.

The prophecy of the seventy weeks of years concerns Daniel's "people," the Jews; and the holy city, Jerusalem. The end of the seventy weeks of years brings "everlasting righteousness". This is a reference to the Second Coming, the event marking the end of the seventy "weeks".

The event marking the beginning of the "weeks" is the "going forth of the commandment to restore and to build Jerusalem unto the Messiah, the Prince." This is recorded in the Bible in Nehemiah 2, as the month Nisan, in the twentieth year of Artaxerxes the King (the date when the Persian King Artaxerxes issued the decree permitting the Jews to rebuild the walls of Jerusalem). We know this date to be 445 B.C.

The next event to happen occurred after "seven weeks and threescore and two weeks" or 69 weeks. This is the equivalent of 483 years (69x7=483). Add 483 years to 445 B.C. and you get 38 A.D. This is when Daniel is told that the "Messiah would be cut off but not for Himself." This prophecy was fulfilled with the crucifixion of Jesus.

After this the prophecy states "the people of the prince that shall come shall destroy the city, and the sanctuary." This prophecy was fulfilled with the destruction of Jerusalem and the temple by the invading Romans in 70 A.D. Thus, the first 69 weeks of Daniel's time period have already been completed.

With the first part of Daniel's prophecy already fulfilled,

that leaves only the seventieth "week." This seven year period begins with a future prince "confirming the covenant with many for one week." This "prince" is referred to by many as the AntiChrist. The covenant he is confirming is the covenant of the Jews with God. How this confirmation of the covenant will happen is not clear, but it may be in the form of the AntiChrist confirming Israel's right to exist (which many countries still do not concede), or possibly allowing the Jews to reestablish temple worship as the Persian Kings did.

In the middle of the seven year period of the seventieth "week," the AntiChrist will cause the Jewish ritual of sacrificing lambs daily on the altar to cease, and sometime thereafter commit the abomination of desolation. We know the sacrifice will be taken away after three and one half years because the word "midst" in verse 27 literally means "middle." The middle of a seven year period is after three and one half years. We know that the sacrifice will be of animals because the word zebach (sacrifice) literally means "slaughtered animal."

Once the AntiChrist makes his deal with the people of Israel, he will be proclaimed a great hero and friend of the Jews. But after three and one half years he will double-cross the Israelis and somehow cause the sacrifice to cease, probably by military means. The Israelis will fight to regain control of their capital city, but it will not be in their hands until after the "consummation," or end.

After the great tribulation, the AntiChrist will be des-troyed as indicated in verse 27 "that determined will be poured down on the desolate." The word "desolate" in this verse can be translated "desolator" meaning the AntiChrist. Thus, at the end judgement will be poured down on the AntiChrist.

Most experts on Biblical prophecy believe that the taking away of the daily sacrifice and the abomination of desola-tion will occur at the same time, meaning that the great tribulation will last three and one half years, the last half of Daniel's "week." I am not so sure that this will be the case. I think that a three and one half year tribulation is one possibility, but there is another possibility.

Daniel 12:11,12

11 And from the time that the daily sacrifice shall be taken away, and the abomination that maketh desolate set up, there shall be a thousand two hundred and ninety days.
12 Blessed is he that waiteth, and cometh to the thousand three hundred and five and thirty days.

Verse 11 of this passage seems to imply that the abomination will occur 1290 days after the sacrifice is taken away. Thus the taking away of the sacrifice, and the setting up of the abomination may or may not occur simultaneously. There is some precedent for this. When the temple was desecrated by the Syrian king, Antiochus Epiphanes, in 165 B.C., he committed his abomination 2 years after he took away the daily sacrifice. Antiochus is written about in Daniel, and the period of time mentioned begins with the taking away of the sacrifice, not with the abomination he committed. If there is a difference in the timing of the two events then the great tribulation may only last 45 days, the difference between the 1290 days of verse 11 and the 1335 days of verse 12. The "blessed event" of verse 12 would seem to be either the Second Coming or the end of the great tribulation. This blessed event will come 1335 days after the sacrifice is taken away.

Whether the tribulation will last three-and-one-half years or 45 days, we will have to wait and see. The nature of modern warfare is such that wars are over in days instead of years. Since this war will be a time of great affliction, it may be that 45 days is not enough to classify as a "great tribulation." It seems, however, that the abomination will be so obvious that everyone familiar with the prophecies will recognize it immediately and will be prepared for the tribulation.

Let's review for a moment what we have covered about Daniel's prophecy. The timing of events will be as follows: a seven year period known as Daniel's seventieth week will begin with a future prince making a covenant or deal involving the Israelis. After three and one half years he will cause the ritual sacrificing of animals in the rebuilt temple to cease, and sometime thereafter desecrate the temple. After this desecration, the world will go through a great tribulation followed by the Second Coming.

Many Israelis believe that we are presently approaching the time of the coming of the Messiah. Not the Second Coming of Jesus, but the first coming of a Messiah who will be the Savior of Israel. While excavating the temple mount in Jerusalem, Israeli workers uncovered the following inscription carved on the walls of the old temple:

Isaiah 66:14

14   And when ye see this, your heart shall rejoice, and your bones shall flourish like an herb; and the hand of the Lord shall be known toward his servants, and his indignation toward his enemies.

Rabbis considered this inscription to be a sign of the coming of the Messiah. Rather than a sign of a new Messiah, it is a sign of the Second Coming of Jesus.

Events involving the temple mount should be watched closely in the future. Recently the temple mount was the focus of conflict when an Israeli soldier described as "mentally ill" stormed the Dome of the Rock Mosque and began shooting into a crowd of worshipers. Several people were killed before the attacker could be subdued. Israel's Chief Rabbinate denounced the attack, saying, "By this despicable act of opening fire on innocent people, the gunman desecrated the holiest site of the Jewish people and removed himself from the Nation of Israel."

Even though this attack was called a desecration by the Chief Rabbinate it does not classify as an abomination of desolation. When the real abomination occurs, it will be in the rebuilt temple in the holy place.

After the attack on the temple mount the Arab world reacted angrily. King Kalid of Saudi Arabia called for a one day strike throughout the region in protest. A Saudi newspaper called for a jihad or holy war to liberate Islam's holy site from Israeli occupation. On the Israeli occupied West Bank of the Jordan River, Palestinian mobs rioted and stoned cars. In New York, the Jewish Defense League condemned the attack, but called the attacker "a hero who tried to liberate the temple mount from the hands of foreigners." As these examples show, both sides view the temple mount as their sacred land and react violently to any disturbance of it.

There are signs of the Second Coming other than the taking away of the daily sacrifice and the abomination of desolation, but these are the ones most often mentioned by experts on prophecy. Now that we have examined them, let's look at the prophecies of Edgar Cayce in connection with Daniel, the AntiChrist, and the Second Coming.

The AntiChrist

Edgar Cayce is probably the most famous psychic in American history. He lived from 1877-1945 and gave over 14,000 "readings," the majority of which were recorded and are still preserved. Cayce's expertise was diagnosing illness, and most of his readings were devoted to healing the sick. Cayce would lie on his couch, go into trance, and after being given only the name and address of the sick person, would give an accurate diagnosis including appropriate remedies. Cayce's abilities were so profound that his fame put him on the front page of the magazine section of the New York Times on October 9, 1910.

Followers of Cayce formed an organization called the Association for Research and Enlightenment to study and research his psychic readings. The A.R.E., with headquarters in Virginia Beach, still exists today and boasts a membership of over 60,000. The headquarters contains a large library, bookstore, and records of Cayce's 14,000 readings.

Edgar Cayce gave approximately 2,000 life readings. These involve reincarnation, personal and business problems, and sometimes prophecy. The readings in which Cayce gave prophetic information are the ones that interest us.

In one of these readings Cayce accurately predicted a real estate boom for Virginia Beach, including the year in which it would end. Years before it happened, he stated in a reading that Norfolk would be the number one seaport on the East Coast surpassing New York. This is now the case.

Another of Cayce's predictions was that Atlantis would be discovered off the coast of the Caribbean island of Bimini in 1968 or 1969. This was fulfilled by a group of divers who discovered large rectangular stones beneath the ocean just off Bimini's shore. Much of the later discoveries involving these stones are chronicled in Dr. David Zink's book, *Stones of Atlantis.* Dr. Zink mapped and explored the ruins and brought forth evidence that these rock formations were man made. Amazing as it is, Cayce predicted the location and the year that the "stones of Atlantis" would be discovered.

Another prediction Cayce made was that a crystal power source would be discovered by scientists in 1958. The main theoretical papers which led to the invention of the laser (which uses a ruby crystal to amplify light) were put forward in 1958. Once again, Cayce was correct as to the year and the event.

The above mentioned fulfilled prophecies show that Edgar Cayce did have the ability to predict the future. This is not to say, however, that Cayce's predictive powers were infallible. He forecast earth changes for the state of Alabama in the 1930's that did not come about. The "sleeping prophet" always insisted that man had free will, and by acting in accordance with God's laws could change the future. Frequently he stated that a group of people praying together could save a city, a state, or a region. This seems to be what happened when Cayce's predictions did not come true.

The Cayce readings contain several references which apply to our study of the AntiChrist, and here is the first of these:

As is indicated in that period where the entrance is shown to be in that land that was set apart, as that promised to that peculiar peoples, as were rejected-as is shown in that portion when there is the turning back

23

from the raising up of Xerxes as the deliverer from an unknown tongue or land, and again is there seen that this occurs in the entrance of the Messiah in this period-1998.

(5748-5)

The wording of this reading is a little awkward, but if examined closely it reveals its meaning. Cayce in the first part of this reading is speaking of the first entrance of Jesus to the earth "in that period," namely 0 A.D. The entrance point was Bethlehem, part of the promised land, or as Cayce puts it, "that promised to that peculiar peoples." The phrase "as were rejected" refers to the rejection of the Jews by God when they were carried into Babylonian captivity. Now the next phrase is the key point. Cayce states that there was a "turning back from the raising up of Xerxes as the deliverer," and that this would occur again during the entrance of the Messiah in the year 1998, an obvious prediction of the year of the Second Coming. This is easy to see, but the reference to Xerxes requires some historical background.

Xerxes was a very powerful Persian King who assembled an enormous army, conquered Greece, and burned Athens to the ground. His army is considered to be the largest army ever assembled in ancient times. Xerxes' rule stretched from Greece to India and included Arabia, the Holy Land, Persia and Egypt. He was described as "lecherous and cruel," and was well known as a desecrator of temples! Sounds very much like the AntiChrist doesn't it?

Wherever Xerxes went, he burned down and destroyed temples established to worship local deities. Preceding Persian Kings had attempted to appease their subject people by respecting local gods, but Xerxes did just the opposite. He wrecked temples in Egypt, Babylon, and Greece. In Babylon, he went into the temple of Zeus, stole a gold statue of the ancient god, and killed a priest who attempted to stop him.

All of this would be enough to show us that Cayce was

alluding to the AntiChrist in this reading, but when you examine the relationship between the Persian Kings and the Jews, the parallels become amazing. The four most important Persian Kings mentioned in the Bible were:

Cyrus the Great (550-530 B.C.)
Darius (586-521 B.C.)
Xerxes (486-424 B.C.)
Artaxerxes (465-424 B.C.)

Cyrus the Great conquered the Babylonians and permitted the Jews to return to the Holy Land and rebuild the temple. Artaxerxes, the son of Xerxes, allowed the Jewish leader Nehemiah to return to Jerusalem and rebuild the walls of the city. The story of this is in the biblical Books of Ezra and Nehemiah. As you can see, the Persian Kings were deeply involved in the return of the Jews to the Holy Land, the reestablishment of the temple worship and the sacrifice, and the rebuilding of the walls of Jerusalem. Considering that the AntiChrist is expected to be instrumental in dealings to allow the Jews to keep Jerusalem and reestablish temple worship, the similarity between the AntiChrist and the ancient Persian kings is striking.

But what about Xerxes? After Darius died, there was some debate as to who would be the new king. Xerxes was chosen because he was the oldest son of Darius, and because he had a kingly look and manner. The Book of Esther in the Old Testament records the history of Xerxes and the Jews. In the Old Testament Xerxes is known by his Hebrew name, Ahasuerus. Cayce describes him in the following paragraph:

Ahasuerus (Xerxes) came to the throne in his early twenties, and was not an uncouth man: yet — with the ease of the conditions and surroundings — being lauded by the princes of the various charges over which the counselors came — he became rather what would be termed in the present as a dissipated man. He was one, though, fair in the general outlook but with a very decided Roman nose (as would be called in the present), with hazel eyes, with fair hair; the weight being a hundred and seventy-six pounds (as would be termed in the present: then called duets). This was the general mien.

(1096-3)

Xerxes was a tall kingly looking man when he assumed the throne, but because of the ease of conditions he gradually eroded into what Cayce called a "dissipated man." It would seem that this was his condition at the time the Book of Esther was written, for the first part of Esther describes Xerxes as feasting and drinking for seven days in his palace. During this drinking bout he ordered his beautiful queen, Vashti, to come and dance for the entertainment of his guests, but she refused. This made Xerxes decide to dethrone her and choose a new queen, since he felt that Vashti's refusal would cause women throughout his kingdom to refuse the commands of their husbands.

So the search went out for a new queen, one of great beauty to be chosen. Ultimately, Esther, a Jew, was chosen. However, Xerxes did not know that she was a Jew, because she had been told by Mordecai, her kinsman, not to reveal this to the King. During Esther's reign as Queen, Haman, one of the king's advisors, convinced the king that the Jews were an evil people, and that they should be destroyed. Xerxes issued the following proclamation:

Esther 3:13

13 And the letters were sent by posts into all the King's provinces, to destroy, to kill, and cause to perish, all Jews, both young and old, little children and women, in one day even upon the thirteenth day of the twelfth month, which is the month Adar, and to take the property of them for spoil.

So after being friendly with the Jews and letting them

work on the rebuilding of the temple begun under Cyrus, Xerxes changed his mind, and ordered all the Jews in his kingdom killed. This is exactly the scenario that interpreters of Bible prophecy have predicted for the end times: a powerful leader will make a deal with the Jews, allow them to reestablish temple worship, and then turn against them after three and one half years.

As students of the Bible know, Xerxes' mind was eventually changed by his Queen Esther, and he did not kill all the Jews. But Cayce was drawing a parallel here of a leader who was a friend to the Jews at first and later changed his mind. One thing to remember in all of this is that Cayce was an avid student of the Bible, having read it cover to cover once for every year of his life. Therefore, he was familiar with the story of Xerxes in the Book of Esther and with the fact that a future "Xerxes" was prophesied in the Book of Daniel.

The following chart compares the traditional view of the AntiChrist with the life of Xerxes and the Persian kings:

Xerxes	AntiChrist
1. Prophesied about in Daniel	1. Prophesied about in Daniel
2. Cruel and lecherous	2. Evil
3. Head of a powerful kingdom of nations	3. Head of a powerful kingdom of nations
4. Allowed Jews to re-build the temple, then ordered them all killed	4. Makes deal with the Jews to reestablish temple worship, and then turns on them
5. Proclaimed as unbeatable militarily	5. Military power
6. Controlled a large area of the world for several years	6. Power for three-and-one-half years in Jerusalem
7. Desecrated temples in Egypt, Babylon and Greece	7. Desecrates the temple in Jerusalem

Xerxes	**AntiChrist**
8. Blasphemed local gods	8. Blasphemes God
9. Ultimately defeated	9. Ultimately defeated
10. Linked by Edgar Cayce source to the Second Coming	10. Linked by Edgar Cayce to the Second Coming

As we see from this chart, Cayce drew an excellent parallel for us with his reference to Xerxes. During ancient times the fate of the world and the fate of the Jews was tied together by the powerful Persian kings, and Cayce tells us that this will once again be the case. But who will this future Xerxes be? There are several possibilities we will now examine.

The Revived Roman Empire

Most of those who write about biblical prophecy feel that the AntiChrist will be the head of a revived version of the Roman Empire, and there are several reasons they believe this. One reason is that the word used to describe the desecrator of the temple in Daniel 9:27 is the pronoun "he" and the antecedent noun is the "prince" in verse 26. In the case of verse 26 the "prince" was Titus, the Roman Emperor who destroyed Jerusalem and the temple in 70 A.D. Many people feel that since the desecrator of verse 26 came from Rome then the desecrator of verse 27 must also come from Rome.

Daniel 7 discusses four kingdoms that will arise out of the earth, with the fourth being the Roman Empire. After the Roman Empire, another kingdom will arise made up of ten kings, who will give their power to another king, the AntiChrist, who will speak words against the saints and hold power until Judgment Day, when he will be destroyed. This future kingdom is described in Daniel 7 and Revelation 13 in identical terms.

Daniel 7:3-8,15-26

3   And four great beasts came up from the sea, diverse one from another.

First World Empire: Babylon

4   The first was like a lion, and had eagle's wings; I beheld till its wings were plucked, and it was lifted up from the earth, and made to stand upon its feet as a man; and a man's heart was given to it.

Second World Empire: Medo-Persia

5   And, behold, another beast, a second, like a bear, and it raised up itself on one side, and it had three ribs in the mouth of it between its teeth; and they said unto it, Arise, devour much flesh.

Third World Empire: Greece

6   After this I beheld, and lo, another, like a leopard, which had upon its back four wings of a fowl; the beast had also four heads, and dominion was given to it.

Fourth World Empire: Rome

7   After this I saw in the night visions, and behold, a fourth beast, dreadful and terrible, and strong exceedingly, and it had great iron teeth; it devoured and broke in pieces, and stamped the residue with its feet; and it was diverse from all the beasts.

8   I considered the horns, and behold, there came up among them another little horn, before which there were three of the first horns plucked up by the roots; and, behold, in this horn were eyes of man, and a mouth speaking great things.

15   I Daniel, was grieved in my spirit in the midst of my body, and the visions of my head troubled me.

16   I came near unto one of them that stood by, and asked him the truth of all this. So he told me, and made me know the interpretation of the things.

17   These great beasts, which are four, are four kings who shall arise out of the earth.

18   But the saints of the Most High shall take the kingdom, and possess the kingdom forever, even forever and ever.

19   Then I would know the truth of the fourth beast, which was diverse from all the others, exceedingly dreadful, whose teeth were of iron, and its nails of bronze, which devoured, broke in pieces, and stamped the residue with his feet;

20   And of ten horns that were in its head, and of the other which came up, and before whom three fell; even of that horn that had eyes, and a mouth that spoke very great things, whose look was more stout than its fellows.

21   I beheld, and the same horn made war with the saints, and prevailed against them,

22   Until the Ancient of Days came, and judgement was given the saints of the Most High; and the time came that the saints possessed the kingdom.

23   Thus he said, The fourth beast shall be the fourth kingdom upon earth, which shall be diverse from all kingdoms, and shall devour the whole earth, and shall tread it down, and break it in pieces.

24   And the ten horns out of this kingdom are ten kings that shall arise; and another shall rise after them, and he shall be diverse from the first, and he shall subdue three kings.

25   And he shall speak great words against the Most High, and shall wear out the saints of the Most High, and think to change the times and the laws; and they shall be given into his hand until a time and times and the dividing of time.

26 But the judgement shall sit; and they shall take away his dominion, to consume and to destroy it unto the end.

This passage describes four beasts who represent, symbolically, four kingdoms on the earth. The first is Babylon which is represented by the lion of verse 4. The second is Persia which symbolically is the bear in verse 5. The third kingdom is Greece represented by the leopard of verse 6, and the fourth kingdom is the one controlled by the AntiChrist. It is this fourth kingdom we are going to examine.

This kingdom is described in Daniel 7:7 as a beast with ten horns, and the ten horns, we are told, are symbolic of ten kings or ten nations. So, the AntiChrist's kingdom will be made up of ten nations. We are also told that it will be exceedingly strong. The AntiChrist is referred to in verse 8 as the "little horn," and the phrase "little horn" is also used in Chapter 8 of Daniel to describe Antiochus Epiphanes, the desecrator of the temple discussed in the last chapter. He and the AntiChrist are very similar characters.

We are told that the little horn will arise, and subdue three of the ten kings, and take control of the kingdom. He will have power for "a time and times and the dividing of time," a reference to the three and a half year period of the tribulation. He will speak great things against the saints and God, and will make war against the saints, and prevail against them until the end when he will finally be destroyed. All of this is written in the following verses of the Book of Revelation:

Revelation 13:1-10

1 And I stood upon the sand of the sea, and saw a beast rise up out of the sea, having seven heads and ten horns, and upon his horns ten crowns, and upon his heads the name of blasphemy.

2 And the beast which I saw was like a leopard, and

31

his feet were like the feet of a bear, and his mouth like the mouth of a lion; and the dragon gave him his power, and his throne, and great authority.

3 And I saw one of his heads as though it were wounded to death; and his deadly wound was healed, and all the world wondered after the beast.

4 And they worshipped the beast, saying, Who is like the beast? Who is able to make war with him?

5 And there was given unto him a mouth speaking great things and blasphemies, and power was given unto him to continue forty and two months.

6 And he opened his mouth in blasphemy against God, to blaspheme his name, and his tabernacle, and them that dwell in heaven.

7 And it was given unto him to make war with the saints, and to overcome them; and power was given him over all kindreds, and tongues, and nations.

8 And all that dwell upon the earth shall worship him, whose names are not written in the Book of Life of the Lamb slain from the foundation of the world.

9 If any man have an ear, let him hear.

10 He that leadeth into captivity shall go into captivity; he that killeth with the sword must be killed with the sword. Here is the patience and the faith of the saints.

As in Daniel, the lion, the bear, and the leopard are mentioned as an allusion to the new empire that will combine all the qualities of the Babylonian, Persian, and Greecian empires. Instead of being called the "little horn," the AntiChrist in Revelation is called the "beast." Power is given to the beast for three and one half years, and power is given him over all kindreds, and tongues, and nations. The beast blasphemes God and those who dwell in heaven, and his kingdom is made up of ten nations (the ten horns and ten crowns) just like the little horn of Daniel. Another parallel development is the reference to war (Who is able to make war with him?). There is no mention in Revelation of the three kings who will be subdued, but Revelation 13:1 does mention that the beast has seven heads and ten crowns. The difference between the seven heads and ten crowns are the three subdued kings.

A clue as to the identity of the beast is given in verse 3. It states that one of his heads will be wounded as if to death, but that his wound will be miraculously healed. This may mean that the Antichrist will receive a head wound and will appear to be dead, but will come back to life. If this happens it will clearly indicate who the AntiChrist is.

The following chart compares Daniel 7 and Revelation 13:

Daniel	**Revelation**
1. Lion, Bear, Leopard	1. Lion, Bear, Leopard
2. Ten horns, ten kings-three subdued	2. Ten horns, ten crowns, seven heads
3. War against the saints	3. Who is able to make war with him
4. Blaspheme the saints	4. Blaspheme God
5. Mouth speaking great things	5. Mouth speaking great things
6. A time and times and the dividing of times	6. Power to continue (forty-two months — 3½ years)

The beast or little horn will be the head of a kingdom of ten kings (three of which he will subdue); he will have the power for three and one half years during which time he will blaspheme God and the saints. The final blasphemy by the AntiChrist will be the abomination of desolation spoken of by Jesus in Matthew 24.

The Common Market

The most popular of several theories is that the Anti-Christ will be the head of the European Economic Community or, as it is known, the Common Market. The main reasons for the popularity of this theory are that the

European Economic Community is composed of ten nations and covers the area of the ancient Roman Empire, as predicted in Daniel.

The Common Market became a ten nation group on January 1, 1981 with the addition of Greece as the tenth member. The ten nations of the Common Market are: France, West Germany, Belgium, The Netherlands, Italy, Luxembourg, Ireland, United Kingdom, Denmark and Greece.

There are several good reasons to think that the Anti-Christ could come from the EEC. Europe holds a pivotal position in world affairs, and united into one force it would have remarkable economic and political strength. The main reason the EEC was formed was to create a unified European economic power to compete with the United States and Japan. This is important because economic control is theorized to be the way in which the beast will gain power over the world. Revelation tells us that no man will be able to buy or sell without the number of the beast on his hand or his forehead, and the number of the beast is 666. One suggested meaning for this is that 666 represents a credit number which, much like a credit card number, each person will have to use when they make a purchase or a monetary transaction. This number could be tattooed on the hand, invisible except when read by a special machine. Such a system has already been developed and introduced as an alternative to the use of cash. It uses three six digit numbers to identify the person making the transaction, and is laughingly referred to by the people who work on it as "the beast." With a computerized credit system a government leader could control all transactions within an economy, and this may be the way the beast obtains world power.

A new economic order will have to be set up if the world economy crashes as it did in the 1930s. Over the decade of the 1970s, third world countries have built up an enormous debt to the industrialized nations. If this debt is not paid it could bring about just such an economic collapse. The EEC would be central to any economic reorganization since it is a trading partner both to the West and to the East.

Politically, there have been indications that Europe is shifting away from the United States toward a more leftist form of government, and this may be one of the signs that Europe is headed for trouble. Disagreements over the installation of U.S. missiles in Europe have brought forth the possible breakup of the Western Alliance. Communists have been elected to legislative positions in several European countries, and even hold cabinet posts in the socialist government of France. The communist philosophy is perfectly tailored to an AntiChrist because of its atheistic bent, and a charismatic communist leader could use Eurocommunism in the same way that Hitler used the Nazi Party to gain power in Germany. Such a leader could mesmerize the people into following his lead away from NATO and into a united Europe with its own government, army, and economic policy. Recently there has been talk of a European Nuclear Force, a powerful weapon in the hands of a United Europe led by a dictator.

Militarily, Europe has become more involved in the Middle East and Africa in recent years. European troops were moved into Beirut in 1982 as part of the Multinational Peacekeeping Force. France sent its troops and planes to Chad in North Africa in 1983 to halt the Libyan invasion of that country. Any type of military or political involvement in the Middle East area by the Europeans should be watched closely in the coming years as a tipoff to a European AntiChrist, particularly any involvement with Israel.

Anti-semitism has increased in Europe recently and that would fit the scenario. There have been an increasing number of terrorist attacks on Jews including a shooting spree at a Jewish restaurant in Paris. Also in Paris, the Israeli airline El Al had one of its ticket counters bombed in an attack that injured seven people. Much of this anti-semitism was motivated by the Israeli invasion of Southern Lebanon. In what many considered the most frightening incident, Italian strike demonstrators shouted, "Jews to the ovens!" as they marched past a synagogue in Rome. These incidents show that the hatred of the Jews fermented by the Nazis in Europe many years ago is still in existence today, and this hatred may ultimately give rise to a European AntiChrist.

The Arabs

The worst enemies the Jews have in the world today are the Arabs. They have said repeatedly that the Israelis are the greatest threat to peace in the Middle East, and that they must be "driven into the sea." The Arabs hatred of the Jews is so strong that most Arab countries do not even admit that the State of Israel has a right to exist. This feeling is understandable since Israel was formed out of Palestine, an area in which the Arabs have lived for two thousand years.

As mentioned before, according to Jewish law, the Jewish temple has to be built on the same site where it was 2,000 years ago in Jerusalem. Right now the Moslem holy place, the Dome of the Rock is located on that site. To rebuild the temple, the Israelis must make some kind of agreement with the Moslems. The Jews might go ahead and build the temple without Moslem permission, but since Daniel mentions a firm convenant being made, at least part of any diplomatic agreement about the temple mount would have to involve the main participants in the struggle —namely the Arabs and the Israelis.

Cayce spoke of the "raising up of Xerxes" as a precedent to the Second Coming. And who was Xerxes but a Persian King? So, Cayce may have been referring to a king from that region. Xerxes ruled from an area that is now on the Iran-Iraq border, so it's possible that the AntiChrist will come from one of the countries in that area. He might enter into an agreement with the Israelis involving the temple mount or Israel's right to exist. The scene would be very much like the one when Egypt's President Anwar Sadat went to Jersualem to make peace with the Israelis. The

AntiChrist would be seen as a great friend like Sadat, but unlike Sadat would later reverse himself.

Also, remember Daniel and Revelation say that the kingdom of the desecrator will have control over the entire world. The Arab oil kingdoms thru their oil have that kind of power. The oil sheiks could wreck the American economy without firing a single shot in anger. They could also devastate the economies of Japan, Europe, and the rest of the free world. Saudi Arabia, for example, makes 120 billion dollars a year on oil sales. At that rate in ten years they could buy every share of stock on the New York Stock Exchange. In ten years this cash flow amounts to one trillion dollars, a staggering figure.

Another fact that would implicate the oil sheiks as a possible AntiChrist is that their lifestyle is very much like that of Xerxes. They maintain harems, just like Xerxes did, and have a life of incredible opulence. Their kings are chosen by family relationships, usually the oldest male in the family succeeds. As we have seen, this is how the Persians chose their kings.

An Arab confederacy like the ten nation group mentioned in the biblical prophecies, is also possible. The Arabs have organizations like OPEC (Organization of Petroleum Exporting Countries), and the Arab League. Recently a group of oil-rich Persian Gulf States began organizing a common defense group. With the amount of weapons they are buying from the United States and their combined economic clout they could be a powerful force in the region. Anyone who doubts this should look at the following list of the countries and populations and imagine them united under one leader:

Syria	8,000,000	South Yemen	2,000,000
Iraq	12,000,000	Kuwait	1,000,000
Iran	34,000,000	Yemen	6,000,000
Saudi Arabia	9,000,000	United Arab	
Jordan	2,500,000	Emirates	255,000
Oman	8,000,000		

The total population of these countries is 80 million or so, much larger than the population of Israel which stands at 5 million. And of that five million, about 1 million are Palestinian Arabs with sympathies against Israel.

Iran, the country in this list with the largest population, is unfortunately one of the most radical of the Arab regimes. The fall of the Shah created a vacuum of power that was filled by the Shiite Moslem leader, Ayatollah Khomeini. Khomeini claims to be a religious leader but is actually a political one. His reign is the type of fusion of church and state that many have envisioned for the AntiChrist. Khomeini is not the AntiChrist, but his rule provides us with a good example of what an Arab AntiChrist might be like.

Kohmeini's regime has been ruthless to say the least. Executions of "dissidents" are carried out on a daily basis, with little cause or pretext except guilt by association. The Revolutionary Guard, Khomeini's elite, have terrorized opposing political factions with regularity. The people of the United States got a taste of their methods during the Hostage Crisis. Fifty-two Americans were held against their will and threatened with death by these fanatics. Only the intervention of the Ayatollah himself prevented the execution of the American hostages.

Khomeini has called for Iranian style revolutions in neighboring Arab countries to overthrow more moderate governments. This is a frightening development for a number of reasons. The assassination of Egypt's President Sadat by Moslem fundamentalists demonstrated that anti-West feelings run deep in the Arab countries and that these feelings can change the political situation.

There are large Shiite Moslem populations in Iraq and Syria, and if these countries were to come under Moslem fundamentalist control, it could create a new Persian Empire complete with a new Xerxes. Along these lines, the Syrian government recently had to use its army to put down a Moslem rebellion which claimed many lives. In Iraq, President Hussein is from a different Moslem sect than the

Shiite, who make up two-thirds of the population. This situation may make his position tenuous in the future.

The Iran-Iraq war has contributed to this instability even further. Iraq invaded Iran and was encouraged by its early successes in capturing Iran's oil rich Kudestan province and the port city of Korremshar. The Iranians counterattacked and forced the Iraqis back into their own territory. The Iranians believing that Allah was on their side fought fanatically and badly defeated the Iraqis. This defeat hurt President Hussein and caused an erosion of support for his leadership in Baghdad. Not only did the invasion show a more militant attitude on the part of the Iranians, but they used the rhetoric of a holy war in describing their actions. They named the invasion "Operation Ramadan" after the Islamic holy month of the same name and stated that the purpose of the invasion was to defeat Iraq and liberate Jerusalem and its Moslem holy sites from Israel.

Iran's victory in the Iran-Iraq war proved that Khomeini's military is a force to be reckoned with in the Persian Gulf. It has added to the prestige of the Iranian Revolution and made Iran more influential in the Arab world. This could help to cause more fundamentalist revolutions and create an Arab AntiChrist or Xerxes in the Khomeini mold.

Besides Hussein in Iraq, the Saudi royal family is also in a fragile position. They are one of the few ruling monarchies left in the world. With a growing educated middle class in Saudi Arabia, the Saudi family will be hard pressed to maintain power. Moslem fundamentalists took over the mosque in Mecca for several days in 1980 before Saudi police forces could capture them. The fear is that a larger revolution could take place and topple the pro-West Saudi family.

A Saudi Arabian AntiChrist would be in a powerful position, since money is power, and the Saudis have more money than anybody. They are using this money to increase the sophistication of their military by buying America's top fighter plane, the F-16, and the early warning radar plane, the AWACs. The sale of the AWACs to the Saudis caused quite a stir in the United States among people who felt the plane was too secret to be given to Saudi Arabia. The United States lost a lot of equipment when the Shah of Iran was overthrown and many did want to see the same mistake made again with the AWACs.

Another problem that arose over the AWAC sale was the Saudis devout hatred of the State of Israel. The Saudis have repeatedly called for a jihad (holy war) to liberate the Moslem holy places in Jerusalem from the Israelis. The Saudis call Israel the "Zionist entity" because they do not recognize Israel's right to exist. The Saudi's hatred of the Israelis is so deep that on checks written in Saudi Arabia is printed "good in any country in the world except Israel."

More and more the Saudis have taken the important role of negotiator between the United States, Israel and the more radical Arabs, such as the Palestine Liberation Organization and the Syrians. In recent years the Saudis again and again have been the go-between in negotiating cease fires between warring Israeli and Arab factions. Whenever American diplomats shuttle between the Syrians and the Israelis, the Saudis are always deeply involved. This could be a perfect position for an AntiChrist. He could offer an olive branch of peace to the Israelis and would be just pro-Western enough to be believed.

Another factor in this is the position of the Saudis as the official defenders of the Moslem holy places. As such, the Saudis would be involved in any negotiations concerning the temple mount and the Dome of the Rock. The covenant the AntiChrist will make may concern the temple mount, so a Saudi AntiChrist would be in a perfect position to fit the prophecy. Recently the Israeli Foreign Minister Moshe Dayan tried to negotiate a treaty with the Saudis whereby the Israelis would keep Jerusalem, but Moslem flags would fly over Moslem holy places. This would have allowed the Moslems to have sovereignty over the holy places. This was rejected by the Saudis, but it shows how important their position is as keeper of the Moslem holy sites.

As mentioned earlier the style of the Saudi kings is similar to that of Xerxes. They are rich, powerful, and to some extent have absolute rule within their kingdom. Xerxes was chosen king because he was the oldest male, and this is the custom today in the Saudi royal family. He was also chosen because he had a kingly manner, another factor in the selection of a king among the Saudis. So Cayce's reference to Xerxes could be a reference to a future Saudi King.

It is easy to see that the Arabs could become incensed enough about Israeli rule in Jerusalem to commit an abomination of desolation. If this happens, it will be a case of history repeating itself. In 165 B.C. Antiochus Epiphanes, a Syrian king, desecrated the temple by sacrificing a pig on the altar and erecting a statue of a false god there. Antiochus is viewed as a type of past AntiChrist and is probably a good model for the future one.

We have examined two possibilities for the AntiChrist's political structure, the Europeans and the Arabs. But there are other possibilities and we will look at these next.

The Invader

On September 25, 1939 (24 days after the beginning of World War II) Edgar Cayce answered the following question:

Q-8 For what real purpose is the present war?

A-8 Read in Daniel, the last two chapters, and see, also the 31st of Deuteronomy — and we will see.

(257-211)

This reading was given for a Jewish man who wanted to know the real purpose of World War II. Cayce repeatedly stated in other readings that the reason for Hitler's rise to power in Germany was so that the Jews would return to their own land, Palestine. Chapter 31 of Deuteronomy, which Cayce recommended to this man, has to do with the return of the Jews to their own land. In this chapter of

Deuteronomy, Moses lectures the Jews just before they are to cross the Jordan River into Palestine.

What Cayce is saying in the above reading is that World War II was the catalyst for the Jew's return to their own land, and the fulfillment of the prophecies of Daniel's seventieth week. At the end of World War II part of the settlement agreement stated that because of the extermination camps and the persecution of the Jews by the Germans, the Jews needed a homeland. Palestine was selected, and ultimately given up by the British to provide a homeland for the Jews.

Cayce also mentioned in (257-211) the last two chapters in Daniel — Daniel 11 and 12. These chapters predict an invasion of the Middle East preceding the Second Coming. The parts of these chapters that concern us are the last verses of Daniel 11 and all of Daniel 12:

Daniel 11:40-45

40 And at the time of the end shall the King of the South push at him (the AntiChrist); and the King of the North shall come against him like a whirlwind, with chariots, and with horsemen, and with many ships; and he shall enter into the countries, and shall overflow and pass through.

41 He shall enter also into the glorious land, and many countries shall be overthrown, but these shall escape out of his hand, even Edom, and Moab, and the chief of the Children of Ammon.

42 He shall stretch forth his hand also upon the countries, and the land of Egypt shall not escape.

43 But he shall have power over the treasures of gold and of silver, and over all the precious things of Egypt; and the Libyans and the Ethiopians shall be at his steps.

44 But tidings out of the east and out of the north shall trouble him; therefore, he shall go forth with great fury to destroy, and utterly to sweep away many.

42

45   And he shall plant the tabernacles of his palace
      between the seas in the glorious holy mountain; yet
      he shall come to his end, and none shall help him.

Daniel 12:1

1   And at that time shall Michael stand up, the great
      prince who standeth for the children of thy people,
      and there shall be a time of trouble, such as never
      was since there was a nation even to that same time;
      and at that time thy people shall be delivered, every
      one that shall be found written in the book.

   This passage deals with an invasion of the Middle East by
a future king. He will enter the glorious land (Israel) and
pass through into Egypt. We know that the verses refer to
the time of the end because the events described in this
section of Daniel have never been fulfilled. Plus, we are told
that the invasion will be at the "time of the end."
   Verse 1 of Daniel 12 shows us that the invasion will occur
at the beginning of the tribulation because the wording of
this verse is identical to Jesus' description of the tribulation
in Matthew 24. It states that the tribulation will be a time of
"great trouble" such as never seen before. Verse 45 states
that the invader will "plant the tabernacles of his palace
between the seas in the glorious holy mountain." This
means he will plant the tents of his headquaters in the land
of Zion (Israel) which in Joel 13:17 is referred to as the "holy
mountain." It is possible that the mountain referred to is not
only the land of Israel, but Mount Moriah, the site of the
Jewish temple in Jerusalem. Thus, after the invasion the
invader will set up his headquarters in Israel possibly in
Jerusalem.
   The military aspects of this war in the Middle East
provide us with clues as to who the invader will be. Verse 43
says that the Libyans and the Ethiopians shall "be at his
steps." This means they will be servants of the invader, or as
it is called in war, allies. This is not surprising since Libya

and Ethiopia are at present bitter enemies of Israel.

Verse 41 states that the lands of Edom, and Moab, and Ammon will escape invasion. These names were used in biblical times to describe what is now the country of Jordan. This fits since Jordan is a traditional enemy of Israel, and would be against the Jews in any war.

One of the most interesting aspects of all this is that both Israel and Egypt will be invaded, and possibly allied together against the invader. Until the Camp David agreement of a few years ago, establishing peace between Egypt and Israel, this would not have seemed possible. Now this would seem to be more than likely.

After Egypt and Israel are subdued, the invading king will be disturbed by tidings out of the North and East, and shall go forth to kill many people. But as verse 45 tells us, he will come to his end, and no one will help him. Whether he will be destroyed by men or an act of God is not made clear, but he will ultimately be destroyed.

The Michael written of in verse 1 of chapter 12 is Michael, the Archangel. He will deliver the souls of all that are written in the Book of Life. Those who have followed the true spirit of the Christ, whatever their religion, will be delivered.

Before this however, a great military power must arise, and defeat Israel and Egypt and this will take a very strong army indeed. There would seem to be only two possible countries in the world that could accomplish this.

The Soviet Union

The Soviet Union has long been a persecutor of Jews both inside the U.S.S.R. and elsewhere in the world. The case of Soviet Jewry has been a celebrated one among free people in the West especially in the U.S. Jewish community. The Soviet government maintains a policy of official atheism, so any group with a strong religious feeling immediately comes into conflict with the government.

Just how opposed the Soviet government is to *any*

religious feelings can be seen by their recent behavior around Easter time. The government sent loudspeaker trucks around Moscow to make fun of Easter and to encourage citizens not to attend services. In addition Soviet television waited until the time period of Easter Mass to broadcast the most popular entertainment programs in order to keep people from attending services.

In Middle Eastern affairs the Soviets are vehemently opposed to the existence of the State of Israel. The enemies of Israel whoever they might be at the time, are invariably supplied by the Soviet Union. This would include Egypt, when they were at war with Israel, and the Syrians today. In almost every Arab-Israeli conflict, it is Soviet-made weapons that kill Jews on the battlefield.

As a result of the Soviets' hatred of the Jews a strong argument can be made for the Soviets being the invader written about in Daniel 11. The Soviet military, which contains twice as many men as the U.S. military, is one of the most powerful in the world. The Soviets have 4,800,000, men in arms as opposed to 2,000,000 for the United States. The Soviets have built a force of 50,000 tanks which would be the spearhead for any land battle, such as an invasion of Israel. The United States has only 11,000 tanks most of which could not get to a battle in the Mideast for weeks. All this does not even include Soviet nuclear capability which is an even match for the United States at the present time. To defeat Israel, Egypt, and the other countries mentioned in Daniel 11 will require tremendous military power. It is a convincing argument that only one country in the world, the Soviet Union, could put that much power in the Middle East that quickly.

The reason for this can be seen very clearly by looking at a map of the area. The Soviet Union is directly north of Israel, which means that the Soviets have very easy access to Israel by land. American forces would have to arrive by air or sea; and outside of planes from U.S. carriers in the Mediterranean, the response would take too long. The United States is too far away from the area to act quickly. The

Soviets on the the other hand could mass troops on their own borders and rush in, as they did in Afghanistan.

Soviet motivations toward the Mideast were clearly shown by their invasion of Afghanistan, a very poor country with no value in and of itself except that it is located near the oil rich states of the Middle East. Yet, the Soviets overran it with reckless abandon. The Soviets have always desired a warm-water port, and that combined with their greed for oil was too much for them to control. So they overran a defenseless country in an act of aggression.

An invasion of Israel might provide the Soviets with similar rewards. The invasion route between the Soviet Union and Israel includes Iraq's richest oil fields. This route includes Iran, Iraq and Syria, three countries with no friendship treaties with the United States. The Soviets might feel that the United States would do nothing to stop them in these countries and by the time the Soviet army reached Israel, it would be too late.

During the 1973 Yom Kippur War, the Israeli army had the Egyptian army completely surrounded and their supply lines cut off. The Soviets, who were Egypt's allies at the time, informed the United States that if the Israelis did not release the Egyptian army and allow it to retreat, then the Soviets would invade the region and rescue the Egyptians. To me this was a particularly chilling development which fit perfectly with the invasion prophecies.

The Soviet army would not include the Red Army alone. It would include the Warsaw Pact countries and possibly some Arab countries as well. Ezekiel 38 and 39 speaks of an invasion of Israel by an army from the North that has been widely interpreted as the Russian Army. Included in the invasion forces of Ezekiel 38 were troops from Peshia (Iran), Put and Cush (Libya and Ethiopia). Libya and Ethiopia were mentioned in Daniel 11 as being allied with the invader, so Ezekiel 38 and Daniel 11 describe the same invasion. Certainly Iran, Libya and Ethiopia would be anti-Israel in almost every case. Ezekiel predicts the invasion force will ultimately be destroyed by God in the form of fire.

One way to determine who this invader may be is to watch who is allied with the Libyans during the coming days. Colonel Quadafi has made no bones about his hatred for Israel, and has caused trouble among the world community by providing a haven for the training of terrorist groups. He, like many enemies of Israel, is Soviet supplied and supported, thus lending evidence for a Soviet invader. Still, Libya would be aligned with anyone who was against Israel, so we can't be certain it will be the Soviet Union.

The events surrounding the 1982 invasion of Lebanon by the Israelis provide some clues as to how the invasion of Daniel 11 may take place. The Israelis swept across the border of Lebanon with lightening speed, in order to crush the PLO, which had occupied southern Lebanon after being thrown out of Jordan. In the process of this invasion the Israelis beat the Syrian Army and Air Force badly and captured the road from Beirut to Damascus, the captial of Syria.

The fact that the PLO, Syria, and the Israelis fought each other is not surprising, but what is interesting is the reaction of the other countries in the world to the war. The United States sent four aircraft carriers and a fleet of 70 ships to the Eastern Mediterranean just to remind the Russians that this was a regional conflict. The Soviet Union immediately dispatched a fleet of its own from the Black Sea and put an airborne division in a southern section of the U.S.S.R. on alert (paratroopers are the first to arrive in any conflict because they can move by air). The Russians put this same division on alert during the 1973 Yom Kippur War mentioned earlier.

When the PLO found itself trapped and surrounded it called for help from the Russians. The Russians did not send troops in but airlifted supplies to the PLO in Beirut. The United States then suggested sending in a peacekeeping force of 1,000 Marines to separate the combatants, at which point the Russians warned the United States that "its Mideast policy would change if the United States sent in its troops," a thinly veiled threat to use force.

The Russians' feelings on this matter can be understood if you think of the same thing happening in a Central American country such as Mexico. If the Russians were to send troops to a country so close to our borders we would be upset too. Lebanon and Syria are not that far away from the Russian border, so the Russians viewed the invasion as trouble in their own backyard.

If all this was not frightening enough, it has been reported that because of the Israeli invasion, the Saudis had contact directly with the Russians for the first time. The Saudis do not have diplomatic relations with the Russians, so this was a very unusual occurrence. If the Israeli's aggressive behavior were to force moderate Arab states like the Saudis to turn to the Soviet Union, the results could be grim.

A future scenario might go something like this:

The Israelis get into a war with their arch enemies, the Syrians. The Syrians have extremely close ties with the Soviet Union including a mutual defense treaty which states that if Syria's borders are violated, then the Russians will immediately send in troops. If the Israelis go to war with the Syrians there can be little doubt that they will violate Syrian territory. With the Russians sending in troops, the United States would be immediately involved as Israel's closest ally. Thus, we have a scenario for World War III.

China

Other than the Soviet Union, there is only one other country that could be the invader of Daniel 11 and Ezekiel 38. That country is China.

Revelation 9:13-16

13 And the sixth angel sounded, and I heard a voice from the four horns of the golden altar which is before God,

14 Saying to the sixth angel who had the trumpet,

Loose the four angels who are bound in the great river, Euphrates

15 And the four angels were loosed, who were prepared for an hour, and a day, and a month, and a year, to slay the third part of men.
16 And the number of the army of the horsemen were two hundred thousand thousand; and I heard the number of them.

Revelation 16:12

12 And the Sixth angel poured out his bowl upon the great river, Euphrates, and its water was dried up, that the way of the kings of the East might be prepared.

The preceding verses of the Bible have been interpreted as referring to an invasion of the Middle East by the Chinese. The Revelation states that an army of 200 million will invade from beyond the Euphrates River, which is in what is now Iraq. Only one country in the world could put an army in the field of 200 million, and that is China. China has a militia of 200 million and a civilian population of over one billion people. China's geographic location is east of the Euphrates River from where we are told the kings of the east will come. In addition, we are told that it will be necessary to dry up the Euphrates River in order that this army might pass. There are dams in place on the Euphrates that could shut off the river's flow. This is something that armies did in ancient times to provide easier passage, and Revelation says it will happen again.

Certain present-day events make this part of Revelation particularly disturbing. China recently flexed its military muscle with an invasion of Vietnam, showing a more aggressive attitude. China has become a nuclear power, having exploded several nuclear devices, and has been working on missile systems, including submarine launched missiles which are invulnerable to attack! This is frightening when you consider that the Chinese could lose 100 million civilian casualties in a nuclear war, and not even bat an eye. They are preparing for just such an eventuality by building one of the most extensive underground fallout shelter systems in the world under their capital city of Peking. Underground tunnels run for miles providing safety in case of a direct hit from a nuclear bomb. The building of these tunnels shows that the Chinese do not consider nuclear war unthinkable, as we do.

Because of the opening of relations with China, the United States has increased its trade commitment with the Chinese. These commitments include some materials with military applications such as heavy trucks. This development prompted Russian novelist Aleksandr Solzhenitsyn to warn the United States not to arm China in hopes of neutralizing the Soviets, because if we armed China we would be "giving away the other half of the world."

Anyone who believes that the Chinese have no interest in Middle Eastern politics should remember that PLO Chief Yasser Arafat and Libyan strongman Colonel Quadafi were in China recently on friendly visits. China has repeatedly taken anti-Israeli positions in UN votes, and has been generally anti-Israeli in all questions of foreign policy. There is no reason to expect their position to change in the future.

The prospect of a Chinese invasion of the Middle East is the most frightening of all. To come overland from China would require an invasion of Afghanistan, Iran, the Soviet Union, Iraq and Syria, unless, of course, China was allied with these countries. This route, including the Kabur Pass in Afghanistan, has been used countless times in the past as an invasion route. The carnage from such an invasion would be the worst the world has ever seen. Nuclear weapons would be the only way to stop such a large army, and this would be an unacceptable option because of the civilian deaths it would cause in the countries being occupied. The Israelis would no doubt use their nuclear arsenal which they call the "doomsday machine," but this would be puny against any army of untold millions. They would be like ants overrunning the landscape.

China's intention to invade the Middle East may have been revealed by recent actions. The Chinese have built a super-highway through the Himalayas to Pakistan. India protested this action to the United Nations as a threat to peace in Asia. The question is: Why would the Chinese build such a road unless to use it as an invasion route? Indeed, for an army of 200 million to move such a long distance, an improved road system would be necessary. The Chinese have begun to put such a system in place.

Is there any evidence in the Cayce readings for a Chinese invasion? The answer is yes!

If there is not the acceptance in America of the closer brotherhood of man, the love of the neighbor as self, civilization must wend its way westward and again must Mongolia, must a hated people, be raised.

(3976-15)

A concept that is constantly brought up in the Cayce readings is that civilization is continuously moving west-ward. Example: First came the Roman Empire, then the British Empire, and today we have the American "Empire," each farther west than the preceding. In the above reading Cayce tells us that if the United States does not live up to its obligations with respect to the love of its neighbors and all mankind, then civilization will move west and the Mongol hordes will again sweep the world. The modern-day Mongol horde is, of course, China.

Since this reading says that a hated people of Mongolia must again be raised, it would be good for us to look back, as we did with Xerxes, at the last time Mongolia was the center of an empire.

In the early 13th century a Mongol tribal chieftan named Temuchin began conquering a large area of Mongolia. As his power grew, he organized a huge, swiftly-moving, well-disciplined army, and assumed the name, Genghis Khan or "Very Mighty King." Genghis expanded his empire to include China, and large sections of Asia. Khan's warriors were particularly noted for their savagery. Genghis died in 1227, and his successors, Ogodei Khan and Kublai Khan increased the size of the empire by further conquest and made *Peking* its capital city. By the late 13th century the Mongol Empire stretched from the Pacific Ocean to the Black Sea and included the area of what is now Afghanistan, Pakistan, Iran, Iraq, Central Russia, Hungary and Poland. The invasion route taken by the Mongols in conquering these countries is the same one that China would have to take to invade the Middle East. All in all Cayce drew an excellent parallel for us.

The question is, has the United States provided enough leadership to prevent the Chinese from becoming aggressive? It is doubtful, and this makes a Chinese invasion a strong possibility, and one we need to watch for.

The possible alignments in such a situation are impossible to predict. It might be the Chinese and the Soviets against the United States and Israel. It might be the United States and the Soviets against the Chinese. Neither the United States nor the Soviet Union could use all their weapons against the Chinese for fear of being exposed to the remaining superpower. A three-way superpower conflict is much more tricky than a two-way one. The result might be so terrible that as Revelation says a "third part of the men" on the earth might be killed, as the Chinese would probably use germ warfare in addition to conventional and nuclear. A Chinese invasion would devastate the entire Middle East and much of Asia.

Summary

It is interesting to note what the Bible says about the cities involved in Middle East conflicts. The destruction of Sidon and Tyre (cities in Lebanon) are predicted in Ezekiel, and these two cities were devastated by the 1982 Israeli invasion.

52

This biblical prophecy has already been fulfilled. More important to the future conflict is the prediction in Isaiah that Damascus will be "taken away from being a city, and will be made a ruinous heap." Damascus is probably the world's oldest continuously occupied city, so that prophecy has never been fulfilled. The area around Damascus would be the central location of an Israeli-Syrian war and would be subject to destruction. It is also in line with the invasion route from the Soviet Union and China to Israel.

There are other possible areas of conflict. Verse 11:44 of Daniel says that "tidings out of the north and east will trouble" the invader and in the end "none shall help him." These might be references to battles in other locations. The invading army will have to take on many countries, as Daniel tells us.

There is considerable debate over whether the AntiChrist and the invader will be the same entity or whether the invader will be attacking the AntiChrist. If the invader is separate from the AntiChrist, then the "Xerxes" Cayce referred to might be the invader not the AntiChrist. He would be seen as a "deliverer" rescuing the Israelis from the AntiChrist, but in fact the Israelis would be trading one oppressor for another.

The possible lineups in such a situation are many. There might be a Russian AntiChrist against a Chinese invader. There might be an Arab AntiChrist against a Russian invader. Or the AntiChrist and the invader might be the same person.

It is impossible to say whether the invader and the AntiChrist will be different entities or what countries they or he will come from. The best that can be said is that all of us should be aware of the prophecies and should keep our minds open to all possibilities as these future events unfold.

Nostradamus

Michael de Nostradamus is the most famous prophet in French history. He lived during the 16th century, and his abilities as a prognosticator earned him fame far and wide. He made many predictions of the future, including some applicable to our time, and it is for this reason he is of interest to us.

Nostradamus was born in St. Remy de Provence, France, on December 14, 1503. His family was of Jewish descent, but was converted to Catholicism when Michael was very young. His intellect soon became apparent to everyone, and so in 1522 at the age of nineteen, he was sent to France's most prestigious college of medicine at Montpellier.

During his stay at school the Black Plague struck Southern France and Nostradamus was pressed into service to fight it. He showed great courage during this time, healing the sick when most doctors had moved on to avoid catching the plague themselves. He traveled for several years, then returned to Montpellier to complete his doctorate.

After getting married and settling down to what would seem to have been an idyllic life in Agen, tragedy struck Nostradamus. His wife and children died of plague, ruining his reputation as a healer. Then the Church began to investigate him in connection with the Inquisition, because he had made some careless remarks about a statue of the Virgin Mary that was being erected in town. He was also suspicious to authorities because he refused to bleed his patients, a common practice at that time. Nostradamus was forced to travel to avoid persecution, and it is during these travels that he first began to make predictions about the affairs of men.

Legend has it that during his travels through Italy he passed a monk on the street. Nostradamus suddenly knelt down and called the monk "your holiness." The monk must certainly have been startled since he was only a swineherd at the time, not a member of the church hierarchy. Years later in 1585, the monk, Felice Peretti, became Pope Sextus V. Nostradamus' amazing powers had allowed him to see the future perfectly.

Presumably because of such flashes of insight, Nostradamus began to write *The Prognostications,* his first book of prophecy, which he published in 1554. Encouraged by the success of his first book, he produced his now famous book, *The Prophecies.* This book was an even bigger hit than his first, and Nostradamus was called to Paris for an audience with the Queen, Catherine de Medici. He spoke with the Queen for two hours and stayed on in Paris for several weeks drawing up horoscopes and offering prophetic advice. Soon the Justices of Paris began to investigate him for his magic practices, and he returned home to Salon. It is there he spent the rest of his days, until he died in 1566.

A revival of interest in Nostradamus began during World War II when Frau Goebbels showed her husband, the German propaganda minister, some of Nostradamus' prophecies that appeared to apply to Adolph Hitler. Dr. Goebbels was intrigued and decided to use them as evidence of Hitler's divine destiny to be ruler of Europe. Goebbels hired an astrologer named Krafft to produce propaganda based on the writings of Nostradamus. The British, fearful that the German ploy would have a negative psychological effect on occupied Europe, developed retaliatory leaflets and had them dropped by airplane over the occupied countries. It is doubtful that this propaganda war had any effect on the real one, but the prophecies were convincing enough to cause action on both sides. From them we can see why:

II-24
Beasts wild with hunger will
cross the rivers, the greater
part of the battlefield will be
against Hister. He will drag the
leader in a cage of iron, when
the child of Germany observes
no law.

Nostradamus purposely wrote his prophecy in vague style to avoid persecution by the Church. Thus the name Hister could easily be an anagram for Hitler. This quatrain (as Nostradamus' prophecies were called) refers to all against Hister on the battlefield, as was the case with Hitler in World War II. Given the atrocities committed by the Nazis during this time, the "child of Germany observed no law" but the law of the jungle. We can see very easily how this particular quatrain applied to Hitler and the Nazis, giving credence to the prophetic abilities of Michel de Nostradamus.

With the rash of gloom and doom prophecies now appearing, it is not surprising that the writings of Nostradamus have experienced a revival. Most of his prophecies involve death, war, and famine written as only one who had seen the Black Plague could have written them. Many of the quatrains are senseless and confusing, but some like the Hister quatrains are accurate, making it impossible to dismiss Nostradamus' abilities entirely.

The following quatrain predicts a tribulation before the end of this century.

II-46
After great misery for mankind
an even greater approaches
when the great cycle of the

56

centuries is renewed. It will
rain blood, milk, famine, war
and disease: In the sky will be
seen a fire, dragging a trail of
sparks.

The end of the cycle of the centuries is the year 2,000, and this fits perfectly into the pattern of prophecies we have seen predicting a tribulation at the end of this century. War and famine are mentioned as expected. In addition, a fire dragging a trail of sparks could be the appearance of a comet as a celestrial harbinger of things to come. Halley's Comet is due in 1986, but this is too early for our timetable, so there may be another comet later towards the end of the 1990s. Another possibility is that this is Nostradamus' description of a missile; something he would not have seen in the 16th century, and therefore would have no way of describing. The following quatrain describes the great famine.

I-67
The great famine which I
sense approaching will often
turn (in various areas) then
become world wide. It will be
so vast and long lasting that
(they) will grab roots from the
trees and children from the breast.

This is a frightening description by which we can see the gloomy tone of the quatrains. Clearly Nostradamus felt we were in for devastating famine, so much so that people will eat the roots from the trees.

A number of the quatrains mention the AntiChrist, and the following hints at an AntiChrist empire.

III-97
A new law will occupy a new
land around Syria, Judea and

Palestine. The great barbarian
Empire will crumble before
the century of the sun is
finished.

This quatrain has been interpreted as describing the birth
of the State of Israel. The century of the sun is the 20th
century, and a "great barbarian empire" will crumble before
this century is through. From this quatrain and others
describing an AntiChrist from the East, people have
predicted an Arab and also a Chinese AntiChrist. The
following quatrain is important in that connection.

X-72
In the year 1999, and seven
months, from the sky will come
the great King of Terror. He
will bring to life the great
king of the Mongols. Before and
after War reigns happily.

The date here, 1999, is of course, very close to Cayce's
date of 1998, a fascinating coincidence to say the least.
During this period a great "King of Terror" will bring back
to life the great "King of the Mongols," and war will reign.
This dregs up visions of the army of 200 million in
Revelation. Nostradamus may have been describing those
verses from The Revelation, as he must surely have been a
student of the Bible. This, however, is pure speculation. In
any case this quatrain comes close to the picture of the
future we have gleaned from other sources.

To sum up, Nostradamus predicts war and famine
toward the turn of the century along with an Asian
AntiChrist. His prophecies predict a comet will appear in
association with these events. Fortunately, we know that if
Nostradamus was right about his gloom, doom, death, and
destruction prophecies, the period following will be the
joyous millennium mankind has looked forward to for so
long.

Earth Changes

After looking at the events leading up to the Second Coming the obvious question is, "What will be the timing of these events?" This seems easy enough to figure out using Daniel and the Cayce readings. If the Second Coming will occur in 1998, then we can figure events backwards from there. Daniel's seven year seventieth "week" ends with the Second Coming, therefore, it will begin in 1991. Daniel's week begins with the AntiChrist making a "covenant with many," probably in the form of a diplomatic agreement allowing the Jews to rebuild the temple on Mount Moriah or confirming Israel's right to exist. The daily sacrifice of animals will be reinstated at the temple site and this sacrifice will be taken away after three and a half years of the seven-year period. So following this scenario, the sacrifice will be taken away in 1994 or 1995.

Once the daily sacrifice is taken away, then the abomination of desolation will occur either immediately, or 1290 days later according to which of the two theories discussed earlier is correct. If the theory of a three and one half year tribulation is correct, then the tribulation will be from 1994-1998. If the theory of a 45-day tribulation is correct, then the tribulation will be in 1998. The timing of these events is based solely on when the abomination occurs, since it marks the beginning of the tribulation.

The tribulation will involve war and the invasion prophecies of Daniel 11 and 12. The conflict will probably be stopped by cosmic events involving earthquakes and earth changes. There is evidence for this in the Bible and the Cayce readings. First let's look at quotes from the Bible:

Matthew 24:29-30

29 Immediately after the tribulation of those days shall the sun be darkened and the moon shall not give its light, and the stars shall fall from heaven, and the powers of the heavens shall be shaken.

30 And then shall appear the sign of the Son of Man in heaven; and then shall all the tribes of the earth mourn, and they shall see the Son of Man coming in the clouds of heaven with power and great glory.

Revelation 6:12-17

12 And I beheld, when he had opened the sixth seal and, lo, there was a great earthquake, and the sun became black as sackcloth of hair, and the moon became like blood;

13 And the stars of heaven fell unto the earth, even as a fig tree casteth her untimely figs, when she is shaken of a mighty wind.

14 And the heaven departed as a scroll when it is rolled together; and every mountain and island were moved out of their places.

15 And the kings of the earth, and the great men, and the rich men, and the chief captains, and the mighty men and every slave, and every free man, hid themselves in the dens and in the rocks of the mountains.

16 And said to the mountains and rocks Fall on us, and hide us from the face of Him that sitteth on the throne, and from the wrath of the Lamb;

17 For the great day of His wrath is come, and who shall be able to stand?

The verses from Matthew are quotes from Jesus, just after He has told the disciples about the abomination of desolation and the tribulation. He tells them that immediately after the tribulation, the sun will be darkened as will the moon. This reference to the sun and moon being darkened occurs in at least half a dozen places in the Bible in Isaiah, Joel, Zachariah, Luke, and Revelation. The cause of this darkening is not revealed, but we can make some good guesses.

Obviously for the sun to be darkened would require some catastrophic event. One that has been suggested is the eruption of many of the earth's 200 volcanoes within a very short length of time. This would throw so much dust and volcanic ash into the air that it would cause darkness at noon-day. This happened in some cities in Washington State when Mount St. Helen erupted.

The verses from Revelation state that the moon will be as red as blood. Dust particles in the air defract light, and this can cause the moon to appear red. Volcanic ash can also cause this effect. When the volcano on the island of Krakatoa exploded in the late 1800s, it set off a rash of sunset portraits in England because the particles released into the air created beautiful sunsets all over the world. The verse in Revelation which states that the "heavens would disappear like a scroll when it is rolled together" implies some type of smoke or dust cloud. When clouds roll in they make the sky disappear in the same way a scroll disappears when it is rolled together.

Other possible causes for the darkening of the sun and moon are solar and lunar eclipses. These are the only times when we are used to the sun being darkened by the moon, and the moon being made red by being put in the earth's shadow. If the poles were to shift (as mentioned in a reading we will look at later), then we would have solar and lunar eclipses that were not expected.

The possibility of a pole shift seems to be implied in verse 13 of Matthew 24 when it says that the "powers of the heavens will be shaken." What are the powers of heaven? In physics they are gravitation, rotation, and inertia. A pole shift would certainly shake these powers. Also Revelation says that "every mountain and island will be moved out of its place," an occurrence that would require a shift of the whole earth causing volcanic eruptions and earthquakes. Interestingly enough earthquakes can also throw up dust and make the sky darken. This occurred in the United States during the great Missouri quake of 1811.

After these earth changes occur, Jesus tells us that "His sign will appear in heaven." His sign may be a cross or a star like the star of Bethlehem. If it is the sign of the cross, it might be formed by planetary conjunctions or some other celestial phenomena. What the sign will be we cannot be certain, but the cross and the star of Bethlehem are His symbols.

The darkening of the sun and moon are the most important signs to look for before the Second Coming. In terms of numbers this particular omen is mentioned in the Bible more than any other as a foreshadowing of the Second Coming —over a half dozen times in the Old and New Testaments.

Now let us turn to the Cayce readings and see what they have to say about the coming earth changes.

Q. Three hundred years ago Jacob Boehme decreed Atlantis would rise again at this crisis time when we cross from the Piscean Era into the Aquarian. Is Atlantis rising now? Will it cause a sudden convolution and about what year?

A. In 1998 we may find a great deal of the activities as have been wrought by the gradual changes that are coming about. These are at the periods when the cycle of the solar activity, or the years as related to the Sun's passage through the various spheres of activity become paramount or [tantamount] to the change between the Piscean and the Aquarian age. This is a gradual, not a cataclysmic activity experience of the earth in this period.

(1602-3)

As to the material changes that are to be as an omen, as a sign to those that this is shortly to come to pass — as has been given of old, the Sun will be darkened and the earth shall be broken up in diverse places — and *then* shall be *proclaimed* — through the spiritual interception in the hearts and minds and souls of those that have sought His way — that *His* star has appeared, and will point the way for those that enter into the holy of holies in themselves. For, God the Father, God the teacher, God the director, in the minds and hearts of men, must ever be *in* those that come to know Him as first and foremost in the seeking of those souls; for He is first the *God* to the individual and as He is exemplified, as He is manifested in the heart and in the acts of the body, of the individual, He becomes manifested before men...

As to the changes physical again: The earth will be broken up in the western portion of America. The greater portion of Japan must go into the sea. The upper portion of Europe will be changed as in the twinkling of an eye. Land will appear off the east coast of America. There will be the upheavals in the Arctic and in the Antarctic that will make for the eruption of volcanoes in the torrid areas, and there will be the shifting then of the poles — so that where there has been those of a frigid or the semi-tropical will become the more tropical, and moss and fern will grow. And these will begin in those periods in '58 to '98, when these will be proclaimed as the periods when His light will be seen again in the clouds. As to times, as to seasons, as to places, *alone* is it given to those who have named the name — and who bear the mark of those of His calling and His election in their bodies. To them it shall be given.

(3976-15)

3976-15 mentions the darkening of the sun which is written about so often in the Bible. Also mentioned along

63

with this is the "breaking up" of the earth by earthquakes, again, just as the Bible says. 1602-3 seems to imply that the changes will be "gradual" until 1998 when the greatest changes will occur. The poles will ultimately be shifted causing the weather to change all over the world. In addition, upheavals in the Arctic will cause volcanoes elsewhere to erupt, and Mount St. Helens might be an example of this. All of these changes will be in connection with a pole shift.

Volcanic eruptions have caused weather changes in the past; in 1815 the Mount Tambora volcano in Indonesia erupted and released so much dust into the atmosphere that the sun's rays were reflected, creating a very cool summer in North America. It was called the "year without a summer" because temperatures were still winterlike in the Northeast well into June. In 1982, the eruption of the Mexican volcano, El Chichon, caused a dust cloud that extended all the way around the world. Scientists immediately feared that the cloud would cool off the earth's weather, especially since the cloud was situated at the equator, where the earth gets most of its heat. Any major change in the earth's weather could cause crop failures and lead to famine, a possibility we examined earlier.

It has been discovered that the earth's polar axis shifts a few feet every year. This shift was named the "Chandler wobble." It could be that this slight wobble in the axis could work its way into a major shift much in the same way that a slight wobble in a spinning top can accelerate it and cause it to fall over after a few turns.

According to Cayce, the last pole shift occurred 50,000 years ago. This information dovetails with the evidence that has been found. In Siberia in the early 1900s woolly mammoths were discovered frozen solid with summer food in their stomachs. Their bodies were so perfectly preserved that experts estimate only a quick freeze could have done the trick. Only a pole shift could have changed the weather so radically and so quickly that their bodies were frozen with no hint of decomposition. The radiocarbon dating of the mammoths put their deaths at between 44,000 and 48,000 B.C., the time period when Cayce says the last pole shift occurred. These mammoths were used by Velikovski in his book *Worlds in Collision* as an example of past catastrophic changes.

In the previous earthchange reading Cayce states that the sun's activity would become of "paramount" importance in this period of change. This must be a reference to the so-called sunspot cycle. Every 11 years the sun reverses polarity on its magnetic field. In between this 11-year cycle is a 5½-year cycle of high and low activity in the sun's energy. The high activity is called the solar maximum. During the maximum year sunspot activity increases dramatically and the weather on the earth warms up. During the minimum year, the sunspots disappear and the weather on the earth cools down. The time span between maximum and minimum years is not always 5½ years, but usually very close to it. During the last solar maximum year, 1980, the sun had the second highest number of spots ever recorded. What effect this had on the earth is not known, but it definitely heated up the world's weather. It may have also had an effect on man's activities and the earth itself causing the changes Cayce referred to.

Here is a list of the estimated solar peaks and valleys for the rest of the century: '80 maximum, '86 minimum. '91 maximum, '97 minimum. As you can see '91, the year we picked as the beginning of Daniel's seven year seventieth week will be a maximum year. Perhaps an upswing in the sun's energy will cause an upswing in the activites of men, too.

In the latter part of the previous reading Cayce states that changes will occur in America, Japan, and Europe. He states that the earth will be "broken up" in the western portion of America. Scientists for many years have said that the San Andreas fault in California was overdue for an earthquake, so any changes there would not come as a big surprise. Cayce also says that the "greater portion" of Japan must go into the sea. This fits perfectly with what geologists know about the nature of the earth's crust around Japan. This part of the crust (called a tectonic plate) is gradually dipping under another section of crust and is therefore called a subduction zone. Of course, geologists believe this subduction will take millions of years, but Cayce seems to imply that it will happen much sooner. Although the reading does state that these changes will *begin* in the period '58 to '98, it does not say all these changes will happen before the end of this century. The phrase "changed in the twinkling of an eye," however, suggests an immediate change for northern Europe. This could be the destruction of dikes in the Netherlands which would flood a great deal of land in a very short time, since much of the Netherlands is below sea level. This comes to mind as the most vulnerable spot for earthquake destruction in Europe.

Part of this reading says that land will appear off the east coast of America. Cayce followers believe that this may have already happened with the birth of the volcanic island, Surtsey, in the Atlantic Ocean. If they are interpreting the reading correctly, part of Cayce's prophecy may have already been fulfilled. Surtsey rose right out of the ocean floor, formed by cooling lava, so in that sense it just "appeared."

Cayce gave another reading about earth changes that makes some very startling predictions about the changes that will occur in the United States.

As to conditions in the geography of the world, of the country — changes here are gradually coming about.

No wonder, then that the entity feels the need, the necessity for change of central location. For, many portions of the east coast will be disturbed, as well as many portions of the west coast, as well as the central portion of the United States.

In the next few years lands will appear in the Atlantic as well as in the Pacific. And what is the coastline now of many a land will be the bed of the ocean. Even many of the battlefields of the present will be ocean, will be the seas, the bays, the lands over which the NEW order will carry on their trade as one with another.

Portions of the now east coast of New York, or New York City itself, will in the main disappear. This will be another generation, though, here: while the southern portions of Carolina, Georgia, — these will disappear. This will be much sooner.

The waters of the lakes will empty into the Gulf, rather than the waterway over which such discussions have been recently made. It would be well if the waterway were prepared, but not for that purpose for which it is at present being considered.

Then the area where the entity is now located (Virginia Beach) will be among the safety lands, as will be portions of what is now Ohio, Indiana and Illinois, and much of the southern portion of Canada and the eastern portion of Canada: while the western land —much of that is to be disturbed — in this land — as, of course, much in other lands...

Q. I have for many months felt that I should move away from New York City.
A. This is well, as indicated. There is too much unrest; there will continue to be the character of vibrations that to the body will be disturbing, and eventually those destruction forces there — though these will be in the next generation.

Q. Will Los Angeles be safe?
A. Los Angeles, San Francisco, most of all these will be among those that will be destroyed before New York even.

Q. Should California or Virginia Beach be considered at all, or where is the right place that God has already provided for me to live?
A. As indicated, these choices should be made rather in self. Virginia Beach or the area is much safer as a

definite place. But the work of the entity should embrace most all of the areas from the east to the west coast, in its persuading — not as a preacher, nor as one bringing a message of doom, but as a loving warning to all groups, clubs, woman's clubs, writer's clubs, art groups, those of every form of club, that there needs be — in their activities —definite work towards the knowledge of the power of the Son of God's activity in the affairs of men.

Q. Is Virginia Beach to be safe?
A. It is the center — and the only seaport and center —of the White Brotherhood.

(1152-11)

Again, as in the first reading we examined, Cayce says that the changes are coming about gradually. But in this reading he says that portions of the East Coast will be disturbed as well as the West Coast. He even predicts the destruction of New York City. What form this destruction will take is not spelled out, but the use of the word "disappear" seems to imply that it will be covered by the ocean. This disappearance is mentioned right after he says that the "coastline of many a land" will be the bed of the ocean. Included in this submergence are the battlefields of World War II, which would include the coastlands of Europe. The oceans would only have to rise a few feet to cover much of what is now the coastland of many countries in Europe and elsewhere. Articles written in the past few years have stated that man's burning of fossil fuels may cause the temperature of the earth to rise enough to make the polar ice caps melt. This would raise the ocean substantially and fulfill the prophecy.

There may be another cause of New York's destruction, however. Very few people are aware that there is a fault running right through the center of New York City. It is inactive at this time, but it might be activated by the earth changes.

Other changes are mentioned in this reading including the disappearance of the southern portions of Georgia and the Carolinas. These areas, like New York City, are only a few feet above sea level and would be in danger of being covered by a rising ocean. In fact, southern Georgia and South Carolina were once the bottom of the ocean, and to this day have sandy soil from the deposits that occurred at that time.

One question we could ask is why would Virginia Beach be safe when other portions of the East Coast will not? One possible reason is that the earth's crust around Virginia Beach is rising at the present time. During the last Ice Age the weight of the continental glacier that covered much of the United States caused the crust around Virginia Beach to sink, and the crust is just now recoiling from that sinkage. Perhaps during the earth changes whatever direction the earth's crust is heading will be accelerated, pushing Virginia Beach up even more.

Other safety areas mentioned are Indiana, Illinois, and southern and eastern Canada. This matches geological evidence, since Indiana and Illinois are very stable areas, and the rock crust in Canada is so hard that geologists refer to it as the "Canadian shield," the most geologically stable area in the world. This reading does state, however, that the waters of the Great Lakes will empty into the Gulf of Mexico, rather than the Atlantic via the St. Lawrence Seaway. Current geological trends show that the crust around the St. Lawrence Seaway is tilting back towards the Great Lakes, and will one day cause the Lakes to empty into the Gulf. Geologists say that this will not happen for many thousands of years, but the trend may be accelerated by a pole shift.

The most disturbing part of this reading is that Cayce states that San Francisco and Los Angeles will be destroyed before New York. Given what we know about the earthquake activity in California, one does not have to be a psychic to predict this. Several major earthquakes occur each century along the San Andreas Fault, and San

Francisco and Los Angeles are built dangerously close to the fault. Cayce states that the predictions for the destruction of these cities should be given as a "loving warning" and not as a "message of doom," but one must admit that these predictions are indeed gloomy.

For those who don't think major earth changes could occur in the central United States, consider the Missouri earthquake of December 16, 1811. It was the most powerful quake in United States history and was felt over a million square miles. It changed the course of the Mississippi River creating new islands and lakes. Naturalist John J. Aububon stated that "the earth waved like a field of corn before the breeze." Eliza Bryan, a pioneer, described it as follows, "About 2 o'clock a.m. a violent shock of earthquake accompanied by a very awful noise resembling loud but distance thunder, but hoarse and vibrating, followed by complete saturation of the atmosphere with sulphurous vapor, causing total darkness." The Mississippi River actually stopped, rolled backwards, and then surged ahead in huge tidal waves.

The most interesting point regarding this awesome destruction is that (as mentioned earlier) the earthquake caused total darkness. The sun's darkening predicted in the Bible may be caused by an earthquake as powerful.

Another interesting point about the earthquake in Missouri is that it created "Earthquake Christians." People were so awestruck by the power of the quake and the threat of sudden death, that they turned to religion. It has been said that "there are no atheists in foxholes," and apparently there are no atheists during earthquakes either.

Cayce tells us in the following reading there will be a purpose behind the earth changes:

Ye say that these are of the sea; yes, for there shall the breaking up be, until there are those in every land that shall say that this or that shows the hand of divine interference, or that it is nature taking a hand, or that it is the natural consequence of good judgements.

(3976-26)

Cayce once again mentions the "breaking up" and says that it will show the "hand of divine interference." One of the Dead Sea Scrolls entitled the "Battle of the Sons of Light and Darkness," speaks of the "Sons of Darkness" being destroyed during the end time by a "hand not of man." This might be a reference to the destruction of the AntiChrist by natural means such as an earthquake; much as Jericho in the Bible was destroyed.

Of course, Cayce's comment on the "natural consequence of good judgement" is a reference to the building of cities on earthquake faults — San Francisco and Los Angeles being the most obvious examples. Men should know better than to build cities in seismically active areas, for sooner or later a major quake will strike.

The destruction would seem inevitable even without the coming earth changes. However, men through their actions can have an effect on the earth changes. Exploding nuclear devices underground and pumping oil out of the ground near earthquake faults will cause the changes to be more severe. Man should realize this. On the positive side, Cayce repeatedly stated that a small group of people praying together could save a whole region. He emphasized that some of the predictions he made were trends, and that the will of man could change the future. Cayce predicted earth changes for northern Alabama in the 1930s that did not occur, so it is probable that people in that area raised their consciousness in such a way as to keep the destruction from happening. Cayce has not been infallible in his predictions of earth changes. Certainly the omens predicted in the Bible are irreversible and will happen regardless of the actions of man, however, man can have an effect on his own destiny.

1998

Up until now we have talked about the political and military events before the Second Coming, along with the preceding earth changes. But what about the Second Coming itself? Will Jesus come in the flesh? If so, where will the Second Coming take place? Once again we will look at what the Bible and the Cayce readings say about these questions. Surprisingly, they are relatively easy questions to answer.

The following section of the Bible describes Jesus's ascension into heaven after the resurrection:

Acts 1:9-12

9   And, when he had spoken these things, while they beheld, he was taken up, and a cloud received him out of their sight.
10   And while they looked steadfastly toward heaven as he went up, behold, two men stood by them in white apparel;
11   Who also said, Ye men of Galilee, why stand ye gazing up into heaven? This same Jesus, who is taken up from you into heaven, shall so come in like manner as ye have seen him go into heaven.
12   Then returned they unto Jerusalem from the Mount called Olivet, which is from Jerusalem a sabbath day's journey.

Jesus ascends from the top of Mount Olive into heaven, and is received by a cloud. Two men in white, standing alongside tell the men of Galilee that Jesus will return "in like manner." The phrase, "in like manner," literally means in exactly the same manner. This means that Jesus will return to Mount Olive, descending exactly as He ascended. Mount Olive is very close to Jerusalem, and the appearance of Jesus there will be seen all over the city, thus His reappearance will be apparent to all the world.

To those familiar with the Scripture His appearance will be anticipated.

Now let's look at what Cayce says about the Second Coming:

Q. Is Jesus the Christ on any particular sphere or is He manifesting on the earth plane in another body?
A. As just given, all power in Heaven, in earth, is given to Him who overcame. Hence He is of Himself in space, in the force that impels through faith, through belief, in the individual entity. As a Spirit Entity. Hence not in a body in the earth, but may come at will to him who wills to be one with, and acts in love to make same possible. For, He shall come as ye have seen Him go, in the body He occupied in Galilee. The body that He formed, that was crucified on the Cross, that rose from the tomb, that walked by the sea, that appeared to Simon, that appeared to Philip, that appeared to I, even John.

(5749-4)

The first part of this reading has to do with Jesus as a spirit entity. Cayce tells us that anyone can be with the Christ spirit if he wills to, and acts in love to make it possible.

The second part of this reading deals with the physical return of Jesus, and even quotes a translation of the verses of Acts we just looked at, stating that Jesus will return even as the men of Galilee saw Him go. So Cayce agrees with the

Bible that Jesus will return in the flesh to Mount Olive. He will occupy the same body He did before, the body that was crucified and rose from the tomb. He will be recognized as Jesus, and so Cayce is definitely speaking of a physical return. These next readings emphasize this point even more:

Q. What is meant by "the day of the Lord is near at hand?
A. That as has been promised through the prophets and the sages of old, the time and half time has been and is being fulfilled in this day and generation...

Q. How soon?
A. When those that are His have made the way clear, passable, for Him to come.

(262-49)

Keep the faith that ye are magnified in the Persian experience, as ye sought for Him who is the light, the hope of the world today. For until there is again the seeking of such as ye not only proclaimed but manifested, he CANNOT come again.

(1908-1)

The quote from the verses of Acts is once again emphasized. Another point is added: Jesus cannot come again until those that are "His" have made the way passable. This point is explained in reading 1908-1, by the fact that there must be the seeking of the Christ Spirit before Jesus will return. This seeking will be the attracting principle that will bring Jesus back to earth. Like attracts like. This is explained in the following readings:

Q. He said He would come again. What about His Second coming?
A. The time no one knows. Even as He gave, not even the Son Himself. Only the Father. Not until His enemies —and the earth — are wholly in subjection to His will, His power.

Q. Are we entering the period of preparation for His coming?
A. Entering the test period, rather.

(5749-2)

Q. When Jesus the Christ comes the second time, will He set up His kingdom on earth and will it be an everlasting kingdom?
A. Read His promises in that ye have written of His words, even as 'I gave.' [Rev. 1:1,2] He shall rule for a thousand years. Then shall Satan be loosed again for a season.

(5749-4)

Q. Please explain what is meant by "He will walk and talk with men of every clime." Does this mean He will appear to many at once or appear to various people during a long period?
A. As given, for a thousand years He will walk and talk with men of every clime. Then in groups, in masses, and then they shall reign of the first resurrection for a thousand years; for this will be when the changes materially come...

Q. In the Persian experience as San (or Zend) did Jesus give the basic teachings of what became Zoroastrianism?
A. In all those periods that the basic principle was the Oneness of the Father, He has walked with men.

(364-8)

A. He will not tarry, for having overcome He shall appear even as the Lord and Master. Not as one born, but as one that returneth to His own, for He will walk and talk with men of every clime, and those that are faithful and just in their reckoning shall be caught up with Him to rule and to do judgement for a thousand years!

(364-7)

We can see from reading 5749-2 that Jesus will not return until the whole earth is in subjection to His will. This is certainly not the case today, and it will take a powerful stimulus for this to occur. But once again, Cayce states that the earth must be ready for Him if He is to return. I believe the key to this change in consciousness by the people of the earth will be the darkening of the sun. It is one of the most important omens — mentioned repeatedly in the Bible as preceding the Second coming. It is written in the Koran, so it will be recognized universally as proof of His coming. Signs such as this will be so incredible that people all over the earth will have only one place to turn for help, to God. The power of millions of people praying will create an attraction that will draw Jesus back to the earth.

The test period mentioned in 5749-2 is happening right at this moment. All of us are being tried on our willingness to subject our will to the will of the Lord. This is the test.

Mentioned in all three of the previous readings is the thousand years of peace that will follow the Second Coming. This is referred to as the "millennium" by the fundamentalists and the "Age of Aquarius" by the New Age people. It will be a period of time unparalleled in human history. Evil will be set aside, and peace among humankind will be the rule. It is written about in the Book of Revelation in the following verses:

Revelation 20:2-4

2   And he laid hold on the dragon, that old serpent who is the Devil and Satan, and bound him a thousand years.
3   And cast him into the bottomless pit, and shut him up, and set a seal upon him, that he should deceive the nations no more, till the thousand years should be fulfilled; and after that he must be loosed a little season.
4   And I saw thrones, and they sat upon them, and judgment was given unto them; and I saw the souls of them that were beheaded for the witness of Jesus, and

for the word of God, and who had not worshipped the beast, neither his image, neither had received his mark upon their foreheads, or in their hands; and they lived and reigned with Christ a thousand years.

Satan will be locked up for a thousand years after which time he will be released for a season. Those allowed to incarnate during this time will only be those who have not worshiped the animal influences. All will realize and accept the existence of God. There will be no more war or hatred. In short, this will be the greatest time in human history.

Let's look at the common points of agreement between the Bible and the Cayce readings. Both agree that there will be a physical return of Jesus at Mount Olive. Both say that this event will be preceded by the sun being darkened and the apperance of an AntiChrist (Cayce says a "Xerxes"). Cayce clarifies this even further by stating that we are going through a testing period at the present time. Finally Cayce tells us that the entrance of the Messiah in this period will be in 1998.

Given Cayce's date of 1998, Daniel's seven year week and all the events mentioned in the Bible we can produce the following chart:

Daniel's Seven Year Period

1991	Covenant between the Jews and the AntiChrist
1994-95	Temple sacrifice in Jerusalem taken away
1995-98	Abomination of desolation
	Beginning of the tribulation
1998	The sun and the moon are darkened
	Second Coming at Mount Olive
	Beginning of the Millennium

The only events in question in this chart are the abomination of desolation, and the beginning of the tribulation. If the abomination occurs in the middle of the period, the tribulation will be three and a half years long. If it occurs at the end of the period, then the tribulation will be 45 days long. This all depends on which of the interpretations of Daniel 12 is correct.

I believe that we can know exactly how the events will unfold and can follow them using this chart. By the end of 1991 we should know whether Mr. Cayce was correct in his date of 1998. The key will be the events surrounding the State of Israel during 1991, and especially any concerning the reestablishment of temple worship and the daily sacrifice in Jerusalem. Recognition of the Jewish State's right to exist by former enemies may also fit the prediction as would any major diplomatic agreement involving Israel. This will begin Daniel's seven-year "week."

After the sacrifice is taken away (in 1994 or 1995), the abomination of desolation and the tribulation will occur. At the end of the tribulation the sun will be darkened as an omen of the beginning of the New Age. Then Jesus will return to Mount Olive, and the millennium will begin. These events should come in 1998.

Cayce gave the following readings to inspire those who might doubt the reality of the Second Coming:

...leave not out of thy faith nor thy hope those purposes that should be the promptings of this individual entity. For when ye walk with Him, in purpose and ideal, ye will find that ye are never alone. Think not that ye or any other individual may be the only one serving a living God. For since His entry into the world, and His making it possible for man to find his way back to God, there has been and will continue to be an increase. For God has not willed that any soul should perish. Though the lights of hope may oft grow dim, in the violence that is created by those who become self-conscious of ability and who use self and others for gratifying of selfish desires, let it ever be said of thee that ye will make, ye will cause the welkin to ring for the glory of the coming of the Lord. For He will one day come again, and thou shalt see Him as He is, even as thou hast seen in thy early sojourns the glory of the day of the triumphal entry and the day of the Crucifixion, and as ye also heard the angels proclaim "As ye have seen Him go, so will ye see Him come again." Thou wilt be among those in the earth when He comes again. Glory in that , but let it be rather the one reason why ye keep the faith, the faith in the coming of the Lord, to call those who have been faithful; that they, as He prayed, "May be where I am, and may behold the glory which I had with thee before the worlds were."

(3615-1)

Q. For some time I have been thinking continually about the coming of the Kingdom on earth and His coming. Has it any bearing upon the lesson? Please give me more light upon the Kingdom and His coming. A. How long has been the cry of those that have manifested in the earth the glory of the Father through the Son, "hasten, O Lord, the day of thy kingdom in the earth!" How have the promises read that the Son has given? "I go to prepare a place that where I am there ye may be also. I will come again and receive you unto myself." Then, as the individual heart attunes its mind and its body activity into that consciousness of the desire for the hastening of that day. Yet the merciful kindness of the Father has, in the eyes of many, delayed the coming, and many have cried even as the parable He gave, "We know not what has become of this man. Show us other gods that may lead us in this day." Yet the cry in the heart and soul of those that seek His way is to hasten that day. Yet, as He has given, in patience, in listening, in being still, may ye know that the Lord doeth all things well. Be not weary that He apparently prolongs His time, for — as the Master has given, "As to the day, no man knoweth, not even the Son but the Father" and they to whom the Father may reveal. The Son prepareth the way that all men may know the love of the Father. And as ye would be the channel to hasten that glorious day of the coming of the Lord, then do with a might what thy hands find to do to make for the greater manifestations of the love of the Father in the earth. For, into thy keeping, and to His children and to His sons, has he committed the keeping of the saving of the world, of the souls of men; for, as He has given, "Who is my mother? Who is my brother? Who is my sister? They that do the will of my Father who is in heaven, the same is my mother, my brother, my sister." So, as he gave, "I leave thee, but I will come again and receive as many as ye have quickened through the manifesting in thy life the will of the Father in the earth." Hence, know that, as thine mind, thine activities, long more and more for the glorifying of the Son in the earth, for the coming of the day of the Lord, He draws very nigh unto thee.

(262-58)

When I speak of possible dates for the Second Coming, people invariably quote the Bible verse just mentioned "as to the day no man knoweth, etc..." and say that no one can know the time or the day. But Cayce goes a little further with this and says that it may be revealed by the Father. I believe that the Father has revealed the year, 1998, to Edgar Cayce and to us through his readings. I also believe that as the time draws near for the event, the timing will become even more clear to all of us. Man was meant to understand and can always learn more through an inquiring mind, and I believe we are meant to know the timing of these important events.

Ultimately, the Second Coming will occur and reveal to all just whom the Father has spoken to. It will be truly exciting to follow events in anticipation of the return of Jesus. All of us will be tested in the crucible before He returns, but the rewards will be great for those who make it to the New Age.

Physical Description of Jesus

When Jesus returns, how will we know him? What will he look like? Unknown to most people there is a physical description of Jesus in the Archives of Rome. This description is contained in a report written two thousand years ago by a Roman, Publius Lentulus, to the Emperor Tiberias:

"There has appeared in Palestine a man who is still living and whose power is extraordinary. He has the title given him of Great Prophet; his disciples call him the Son of God. He raises the dead and heals all sorts of diseases.

"He is a tall, well-proportioned man, and there is an air of severity in his countenance which at once attracts the love and reverence of those who see him. His hair is the color of new wine from the roots to the ears, and thence to the shoulders it is curled and falls down to the lowest part of them. Upon the forehead, it parts in two after the manner of Nazarenes.

"His forehead is flat and fair, his face without blemish or defect, and adorned with a graceful expression. His nose and mouth are very well proportioned, his beard is thick and the color of his hair. His eyes are gray and extremely lively.

"In his reproofs, he is terrible, but his exhortations and instructions, amiable and courteous. There is something wonderfully charming in his face with a mixture of gravity. He is never seen to laugh, but has been observed to weep.*

---

*Author's Note: The Cayce readings say He did laugh and quite often.

81

He is very straight in stature, his hands large and spreading, his arms are very beautiful. He talks little, but with a great quality and is the handsomest man in the world."

The description of Jesus in the Cayce readings agrees with the one above:

Q. Please give a physical description of Jesus.
A. A picture (of Jesus) that might be put on canvas... would be entirely different from all those that have depicted the face, the body, the eyes, the cut of the chin, and the lack entirely of the Jewish or Aryan profile. For these were clear, clean ruddy. Hair almost like of David, a golden brown, yellow red. (5354) The Master's hair is most red, inclined to be curly in portions yet not feminine or weak-*strong,* with piercing eyes that are blue or steel-gray.

(5749-1).

In addition we are told in other readings that Jesus wore a pearl gray robe, thus forming a complete picture of a tall well-proportioned man wearing a pearl gray robe and having reddish brown hair and steel gray eyes. This is the Jesus we will see when He returns.

The Last Jubilee

In 1947 two Bedouin shepherds were tending their flocks by the northwest shores of the Dead Sea. One of their goats wandered into a nearby cave, and one of the shepherds tossed in a rock to chase the wayward goat out. The rock apparently shattered something because the sound of breaking pottery was heard. The Bedouin entered the cave to discover what had been broken. He found eight jars (one broken), and in one of the jars he found seven antique scrolls. Thinking they might be valuable he eventually took them to an antique dealer in Jerusalem, and offered to sell the scrolls for twenty pounds. The dealer refused, thinking the price too high, and the Bedouin took the scrolls to another dealer who bought them. Ultimately the scrolls were discovered to be two thousand years old and were undoubtedly the most sensational archeological find of this century. They, along with the other scrolls which were discovered later in the same area, became known as the Dead Sea Scrolls.

The discovery of the scrolls set off much archeological activity in the area of Qumran, not far from where they were discovered. A group of ruins were excavated about a mile from the cave where the first scrolls were found. Coins found in the ruins were dated from 125 B.C. to 68 A.D. From this and other evidence archeologists decided that the writers of the scrolls lived in this community and put the scrolls in the caves to save them from the Roman invasion of Palestine in 68 A.D.

Much debate began about who the people of the Qumran community were. Because the scrolls were Hebrew scriptures including the Book of Isaiah, the community was obviously a Hebrew sect. Most scholars now believe that the people who occupied the community of Qumran were members of a pious monastic group known as the Essenes. The rules of conduct printed in the scrolls were essentially Essene, and the ancient historian Pliny places an Essene community at the exact location of the Qumran ruins on the Dead Sea. From this evidence most scholars are now convinced that the scrolls were the property of the Essenes.

Most of what we know about the Essenes comes to us from the first century historian, Josephus. The Essenes were a puritan community to which one could not be a member without passing rigorous tests. The trial period was three years, at which time the community would decide whether the prospective member could join. At the time of joining a member turned all his property over to the members of the sect to be shared equally.

The Essenes participated in strict religious discipline. Some members of the sect did not believe in marriage and rejected all sexual conduct. Others believed in marriage as necessary for continuation of life, and all believed in the controlling of passions as necessary for a spiritual life. As part of this life they arose before sunrise and before dealing with the matters of the day, joined in joyous prayers as the sun rose. They prayed before and after meals, and lived a life of dedication today only associated with monasteries.

The importance of the Essenes to us is their close association with John the Baptist and later with Jesus. Water was one of the Essenes most important symbols and John, as an Essene, incorporated it into his name. Other than the baptismal ritual of John, the Essenes believed in bathing every day, something that was very unusual at that time. Of course, the most famous baptism by John was the baptism of Jesus. This connects Jesus with the Essenes because baptism was definitely an Essene ritual. Equally strong evidence is found in the fact that the baptism occurred in an area not far from the Essene community. There is no doubt, however, that John was much more the Essene than Jesus, for John believed in the letter of the law while Jesus was the embodiment of the spirit of the law.

The following paragraph from the historian Josephus gives us an idea of just what type of people the Essenes were:

> "And truly, as for other things, they do nothing but according to the injunctions of their curators; only these two things are done among them at every one's own free will, which are, to assist those that want it, and to show mercy; for they are permitted of their own accord to afford succour to such as deserve it, when they stand in need of it, and to bestow food on those that are in distress; but they cannot give anything to their kindred without the curators. They dispense their anger after a just manner, and restrain their passion. They are eminent for fidelity, and rate the ministers of peace; whatsoever they say also is firmer than an oath; but swearing is avoided by them, and they esteem it worse than perjury; for they say that he who cannot be believed without swearing by God, is already condemned. They also take great pains in studying the writings of the ancients, and choose out of them what is most for the advantage of their soul and body..."[1]

This is the traditional historical view of the Essenes. The Edgar Cayce readings give a different view, making them much more important in the life of Jesus than traditional history would have us believe.

Cayce tells us that the Essenes were a mystical brotherhood organized for the specific purpose of paving the way for the entrance of Christ into the world. The Essenes' purpose was to purify themselves in order to prepare a virgin who would be a pure channel for the birth of the Christ Child. The readings say that the word Essene means

[1] Flavius Josephus, Selections from His Works, Abraham Wasserstein, Viking Press, New York.

"expectancy." Namely, the expectant birth of the Christ child.

Twelve young girls were chosen as possible channels for the birth, Mary being one of the twelve. Not that the Essenes would choose the girl, but that they might help provide a group from which God would choose one to be the channel for the birth. This would involve an attraction principle much in the same way that the subjection of the whole earth to His Will will attract Jesus the second time. A pure enough channel would attract the spirit of Jesus. As Mary climbed the steps to the altar during the Essene's sunrise worship one day, an angel appeared to the congregation and announced that Mary was the chosen one. Later, after the birth when the Holy family fled into Egypt, members of the Essenes provided protection and guidance along the journey.

What does all this have to do with the Second Coming? The Essenes were a very spiritual group closely associated with Jesus during the time of His entrance to the earth plane in the first century. They knew of the entrance of Jesus ahead of time, and according to Josephus were renowned for their ability to prophesy the future.

Is it possible, then, that the Dead Sea Scrolls, written by Essene prophets, could apply to the Second Coming of Jesus? The Essenes were very familiar with the cycles of the ages and believed that each change in the cycle was accompanied by great changes within the earth. It is possible that some of the Essenes had visions which they believed to be of the immediate future, but were actually of the far distant future. It seems an incredible coincidence that the discovery of the Dead Sea Scrolls occurred at the exact time Israel was being founded (1947-48). Perhaps these scrolls were meant to be found during this time to give us a greater understanding of the past and the future.

With this possibility in mind we will examine one of the Dead Sea Scrolls entitled "The Last Jubilee." (I have chosen three sections of the Scroll, rather than the entire Scroll, which is of some length.) The Scroll is about the "Last

Days" during which time it says, a "Melchizedek redivivus" (reincarnate) will appear and destroy Belial (Satan) and lead the children of God to eternal forgiveness.*

WHEN, THEREFORE, THE SCRIPTURE SPEAKS OF A DAY OF ATONEMENT to be observed in the seventh month, of the tenth day of that month (Lev.25.9) WHAT IS MEANT, in an eschatological sense, IS THAT this final Jubilee will be marked BY A DAY ON WHICH ALL THE CHILDREN OF LIGHT AND ALL WHO HAVE CAST THEIR LOT WITH (THE CAUSE OF) RIGHTEOUSNESS WILL ACHIEVE FORGIVENESS OF THEIR SINS, (WHEREAS THE WICKED WILL REAP THEIR DESSERTS AND BE BROUGHT TO AN END.)

THERE IS A FURTHER REFERENCE TO THIS FINAL JUDGEMENT IN THE CONTINUATION OF THE VERSE FROM THE PSALTER. How long, we read, will you go judging unjustly and showing partiality to the wicked? Selah (Ps.7.9) THE ALLUSION IS TO BELIAL AND THE SPIRITS OF HIS ILK — THAT IS TO (elders who sit in assides but () DEFY GOD'S STATUTES IN ORDER TO PER (FECT JUSTICE). The future KING of Righteousness — that is, MELCHIZEDEK redivivus — WILL EXECUTE (UPON THEM) GOD's AVENGING JUDGEMENT, AND at the same time DELIVER (THE JUST) FROM THE HANDS OF BELIAL AND ALL (THOSE) SPIRITS OF HIS ILK. WITH ALL THE ANGELS (OF RIGHTEOUSNESS) AT HIS AID, HE WILL (BLA)ST (THE COUNCIL OF) BELIAL (TO DESTRUCTION). But the faithful, as the Psalmist says, will return to (their) eminence (ibid), THE EMINENCE IN QUESTION BEING THE (DESTINATION) OF ALL WHO ARE INDEED CHILDREN OF GOD.

*The words in capitals are the words of the scroll itself, while the words not capitalized are filled in by Theodor Gaster in his book, *The Dead Sea Scriptures*.

At that time, IT WILL BE FROM BELIAL, not from God, THAT MEN WILL TURN AWAY IN REBELLION, AND THERE WILL (BE A RE-ESTABLISHMENT OF THE REIGN OF RIGHTEOUSNESS, PERVERSITY BEING CONFOUNDED) BY THE JUDGEMENTS OF GOD. THIS IS WHAT SCRIPTURE IMPLIES IN THE WORDS, "WHO SAYS TO ZION, YOUR GOD HAS NOT CLAIMED HIS KINGDOM!" (Isa.52.7) THE TERM ZION THERE DENOTING THE TOTAL CONGREGATION OF THE "SONS OF RIGHTEOUSNESS" THAT IS, THOSE WHO MAINTAIN THE COVENANT AND TURN AWAY FROM THE POPULAR TREND, AND YOUR GOD SIGNIFYING (THE KING OF RIGHTEOUSNESS, ALIAS MELCHIZEDEK REDIVIVUS, WHO WILL DEST)ROY BELIAL.

OUR TEXT SPEAKS ALSO OF SOUNDING A LOUD TRUMPET BLAST THROUGHOUT THE LAND ON THE TENTH DAY OF THE SEVENTH MONTH (lev.25.9). (AS APPLIED TO THE LAST DAYS, THIS REFERS TO THE FANFARE WHICH WILL THEN BE SOUNDED BEFORE THE MESSIANIC KING.)[2]

Melchizedek was a priest described in the Bible as an eternal being. It says that he had no "beginning of days" and no end of life, that is, he was not born of woman and did not die, but ascended into heaven.

The Cayce readings tell us that Melchizedek was a previous incarnation of Jesus. The Book of Hebrews supports this when it says that Jesus was a "priest after the order of Melchizedek." This Melchizedek-Jesus link is very important because, if Melchizedek was a previous incarnation of Jesus, then this scroll could be describing the Second Coming of Jesus, the *Melchizedek redivivus* (reincarnate).

---

[2] *The Dead Sea Scriptures,* Theodor H. Gaster, Anchor Books, Garden City, NY, 1976.

The Essene who wrote this Scroll was aware that Melchizedek would come back and become the Christ. He may have seen a vision of the future which he believed to be the first coming of Jesus, but which was instead a vision of the Second Coming. This, of course, assumes that the Scroll was written before the recognition of Jesus as the Christ. All this may seem like an unusual possibility, but there is evidence to support it.

A "Jubilee" is the 50th year of a fifty-year period which has special significance for the Jews. This fiftieth year begins on the tenth day of the seventh month. This is the day designated each year as the Day of Atonement, the holiest day of the year for the Jews. The writer of the "Last Jubilee" believed this fifty-year period would conclude with the arrival of a Messianic King on the Day of Atonement.

The state of Israel was founded in 1948. The Cayce readings state that the Second Coming will occur in 1998. Could this last Jubilee be the fifty year period of the existence of Israel before the Second Coming? (1948 + 50 = 1998) Certainly the Second Coming would fit the description of a "final judgment" in the Last Jubilee scroll.

The Jubilee year in the Jewish calendar is what is known as a sabbatical year. A sabbatical year occurs every seven years, but only every seventh sabbatical year is a Jubilee year. During the sabbatical year, Jews are not supposed to plant crops or collect debts. They are supposed to release their debtors of all debts and release all captives which they might have. The sabbatical year was of such great importance to the Jews that the failure to observe it caused them to be led into the Babylonian captivity.

Leviticus 25:8-12

8 And thou shalt number seven sabbaths of years unto thee, seven times seven years; and the space of the seven sabbaths of years shall be unto thee forty and nine years.

9   Then shalt thou cause the trumpet of the Jubilee to sound on the tenth day of the seventh month, in the Day of Atonement shall ye make the trumpet sound throughout all your land.

10   And ye shall hallow the fiftieth year, and proclaim liberty throughout all the land unto all the inhabitants thereof; it shall be a jubilee unto you; and ye shall return every man unto his possession, and ye shall return every man unto his family.

11   A jubilee shall that fifieth year be unto you; ye shall not sow, neither reap that which groweth of itself in it, nor gather in it the grapes of thy vine unpruned.

12   For it is the jubilee, it shall be holy unto you; ye shall eat the increase thereof out of the field.

The Jubilee year or any other sabbatical year does not begin until the first day of the seventh month of the religious year. This is because the religious year begins in the spring, but the secular year does not begin until the first day of the seventh month of the religious calendar. This is confusing, so just think of the first day of the seventh month as the Jewish New Year.

There are three Jewish holidays in the fall during this seventh month. They are: the Feast of the Trumpets, first day of the seventh month; Day of Atonement, tenth day of the seventh month; and the Feast of Tabernacles, 15th day of the seventh month. The Day of Atonement is the day that the high priest enters the holy of holies in the temple and sprinkles the blood of the sacrifice on the mercy seat of the ark of the covenant. This fact is very important to the evidence we are going to look at in support of our theory about the scroll. The symbolism of the Day of Atonement will provide much of the background we will examine.

Even more important than this, however, is the trumpet blast which begins each 50th Jubilee year Day of Atonement. This can be seen from Jesus' description of the Second Coming in Matthew 24:30-31:

30   And there shall appear the sign of the Son of Man in heaven; and then shall all the tribes of the earth mourn, and they shall see the Son of Man coming in the clouds of heaven with power and great glory.

31   And He shall send His angels with a great sound of a trumpet, and they shall gather together his elect from the four winds from one end of heaven to the other.

As Jesus returns to the earth there will be the sound of a trumpet blast. Could this be the trumpet blast of the Last Jubilee? This, of course, would mean that the Second Coming would occur on the Day of Atonement in the fall of 1998. Thus, from the Last Jubilee Scroll and the prophecies of Edgar Cayce, we may know the approximate date of the Second Coming.

So far we have seen that the fifty-year period of the Jewish state and Cayce's date for the Second Coming are the same, and that both the Jubilee year and the Second Coming begin with a trumpet blast. These facts, by themselves, could be mere coincidence. But there is more evidence.

The Book of Revelation is primarily concerned with future events relating to the Second Coming. In Chapters 8 through 11 these events are symbolized by seven trumpets. I believe these trumpets could stand for the seven years of Daniel's seventieth "week." Since each secular Jewish New Year begins with the Feast of the Trumpets, the seven trumpets could symbolize seven years. Most important to us, however, is that when the seventh trumpet sounds in Revelation 11, the temple of God is opened up, and the Ark of the Covenant is seen. The only time the Ark of the Covenant is seen in the temple in Jerusalem is on the Day of Atonement. So, the sounding of the seventh trumpet (which symbolizes the Second Coming) is related to the Day of

Atonement, not only through the trumpet blast, but through the viewing of the Ark of the Covenant. And this is not the only connection between the Day of Atonement and Jesus. The Book of Hebrews relates the two very strongly in the following verses:

Hebrews 9:7-12

7   But into the second (Holy of Holies) went the high priest alone once every year, not without blood, which he offered for himself, and for the errors of the people.

8   The Holy (spirit) thus signifying that the way into the holiest of all was not yet made manifest, while the first tabernacle was yet standing.

9   Which was a figure for the time then present, in which were offered both gifts and sacrifices that could not make him that did the service perfect, as pertaining to the conscience;

10 Which stood only in foods, and drinks, and various washings, and carnal ordinances, imposed on them until the time of reformation.

11 But Christ being come as high priest of good things to come, by a greater and more perfect tabernacle, not made with hands, that is to say, not of this building.

12 Neither by the blood of goats and calves, but by his own blood he entered in once into the holy place, having obtained eternal redemption for us.

In verse 7 the writer of the Hebrews explains to us that once a year the high priest enters the holy of holies to offer calves blood for the sins of the Jewish people. Jesus, when He came, made this unnecessary by "his perfect tabernacle," His body and spirit. By "His own blood" Jesus entered the holy place in heaven not in the temple.

All this shows that Jesus' crucifixion was symbolically related to the Day of Atonement. This symbolism is so strong that at the moment Jesus died on the cross, the veil in the temple which separated the holy place from the holy of holies was torn in two (Matthew 27:51). Thus Jesus opened the way for all mankind to enter the holy of holies within themselves through prayer and meditation. This tearing of the veil at the crucifixion connects Jesus directly with the Day of Atonement, since the veil is passed only on that day.

The ninth chapter of Daniel is one of the key chapters in the Bible dealing with Second Coming prophecy. Verse 24 of that chapter states that "seventy weeks" (or years) are determined "to make an end to iniquity," this "end" occurs at the time of the Coming of the Messiah. The phrase that is translated "make an end to iniquity" literally means "atone for sins." The Hebrew word used is "Kaphar" which means "atone for." This statement that at the time of the Second Coming all sins will be atoned for, could be interpreted as a reference to the Day of Atonement, especially given the other evidence we have see.

Another important perspective in this is the way great events in Jewish history have revolved around the high holy days of autumn. When the Jews left captivity in Babylon and began to return to Jerusalem, their main goal was to rebuild the temple and reestablish the ritual sacrifice and worship. When the sacrifice was restored, it was begun on the first day of the seventh month, the Jewish New Year. Many years later a revival under Ezra was begun on the same day. Two thousand years later in 1973, a war between the Arabs and Israelis was fought on the Day of Atonement, and thus named the Yom Kippur (Day of Atonement) War.

The most important fact in these examples is that after their return from the Babylonian captivity, the Jews restarted the sacrifice on the first day of the seventh month. Even though the temple was not rebuilt at that time, they erected the altar and began the daily sacrifice. This is important because the Jewish people are deeply steeped in religious tradition.

Once again the Jews have returned to the Holy Land from exile, and one of their concerns is to rebuild the temple. Since we know from the prophecies studied earlier that they will restart the ritual sacrifice, and since we know that they always follow tradition, it seems highly likely that they will begin the sacrifice on the first day of the seventh month as they did two thousand years ago. It is my belief that this restarting of the ritual sacrifice could be the beginning of Daniel's seven-year seventieth week. If the Second Coming occurs at the end of this seven year period, the Second Coming will fall in the seventh month, almost exactly on the Day of Atonement, which is the tenth day of the seventh month. This would place the reestablishment of the sacrifice in the fall of 1991, and the Second Coming in the fall of 1998, on the Day of the Atonement. Even if the reestablishment of the sacrifice is not the beginning of Daniel's seven-year period, there is little doubt that the sacrifice will start on the first day of the seventh month of some year. The Jewish elders are too steeped in the tradition and history of their people to do otherwise.

We have been examining Bible verses so far for evidence of a Second Coming during the high holy days, but is there any clue about such an event in the Cayce readings? I think so. Read through this reading we have seen before:

> As to the material changes that are to be as an omen, as a sign to those that this is shortly to come to pass — as has been given of old, the sun will be darkened and the earth shall be broken in diverse places — and then shall be proclaimed — through the spiritual interception in the hearts and minds and souls of those that have sought His way — that His star has appeared, and will point the way for those that enter into the holy of holies in themselves.
>
> (3976-15)

The phrase the "holy of holies within themselves" refers to those who pray and meditate. What is interesting is that

Cayce chose to use this phrase in referring to the period of time after the sun is darkened. It is clear from Matthew 24 that the Second Coming will occur immediately after the darkening of the sun, and it is here that Cayce mentions the holy of holies. This could be interpreted as an oblique reference to the Day of Atonement, given all the other evidence.

Another possible Cayce reference to a Day of Atonement Second Coming comes in a reading we examined earlier. When asked what the purpose of the Second World War was, Cayce told the person to read the 31st Chapter of Deuteronomy, and "we will see." Part of this chapter has to do with the return of the Jews to the Holy land which we have already seen. In addition, there are two verses that are as follows:

Deuteronomy 31:10-11

10   And Moses commanded them, saying, At the end of every seven years, in the solemnity of the year of release, in the Feast of Tabernacles,

11   When all Israel is come to appear before the Lord thy God in the place which he shall choose, thou shalt read this law before all Israel in their hearing.

The time mentioned in these verses is the 15th day of the seventh month, right at the beginning of the sabbatical year. As every Jubilee year is a sabbatical year, this would point to the possibility of the year being a Jubilee year. And since the Feast of Tabernacles is only 5 days after the Day of Atonement, Cayce could be referring to a future Jubilee. This may be stretching the point a bit, but it does fit with all the other evidence.

The final Bible chapter in this web of evidence is Zachariah 14. It mentions the return of Jesus to Mount Olive, and a battle involving many nations for Jerusalem. The part that interests us has to do with the Feast of the

Tabernacles and the time period after the Second Coming. It reads as follows:

Zachariah 14:16-19

16   And it shall come to pass that every one that is left of all the nations which came against Jerusalem shall even go up from year to year to worship the King, the Lord of hosts, and to keep the Feast of Tabernacles.

17   And it shall be that whoever will not come up of all the families of the earth unto Jerusalem to worship the King, the Lord of hosts, even upon them shall be no rain.

18   And if the family of Egypt go not up, and come not, that have no rain, there shall be the plague, with which the Lord will smite the nations that come not up to keep the Feast of Tabernacles.

19   This shall be the punishment of Egypt, and the punishment of all nations that come not up to keep the Feast of Tabernacles.

The important thing to keep in mind is that these verses are describing events *after* the Second Coming. The verses previous to these have set the stage by describing the events of the Second Coming. Now Zachariah is telling us that during the millennium any country that does not come to Jerusalem to celebrate the Feast of Tabernacles will not find favor in God's sight. Why would the people of the world be celebrating an essentially Jewish holiday *after* the Second Coming? Could it be that they will be celebrating an event that coincides with the Feast of the Tabernacles? If the Second Coming is on the Day of Atonement, then the Feast of Tabernacles might be the date used to celebrate, since it is only five days after the Day of Atonement. There would be no need to have a Day of Atonement anymore since as

Hebrews has told us, Jesus substituted His blood on the cross for the blood of the sacrifice sprinkled on the holy of holies. To me it makes no sense for people to be celebrating the Feast of Tabernacles after the Second Coming unless the Second Coming itself occurred around the same time of year.

An interesting phenomenon has begun to appear in recent years in Jerusalem, and *Time* magazine describes it as follows:

"As the end of the world nears, according to the Biblical prophet Zachariah, visitors from many nations will gather each year in Jerusalem to worship the king, the Lord almighty, and to celebrate the Feast of Tabernacles. These words took life last week (October 1981) as 3,000 people from 35 countries celebrated tabernacles, or sukkoth, with parades, cookouts and musical services in one of the holy city's most spectacular religious events of the year. Significantly, the celebrants were Christians."

Fascinating, isn't it? Christians have already begun to celebrate the Feast of Tabernacles! *Time* says of the people involved, "Virtually all are millenarians, who believe that Zionism is part of God's design for the days preceding the Second Coming of Jesus Christ." Already it seems that preparations are being made for the Second Coming.

Now to review some of the key points of this chapter:

1. The Last Jubilee scroll tells us that a Melchizedek (reincarnate) will return on the Day of Atonement during a Jubilee year (50th) to destroy all evil and establish righteousness.

2. The Edgar Cayce readings say that Melchizedek was a previous incarnation of Jesus.

3. The Jewish state was founded in 1948, so its Jubilee year will be 1998.

4. The Edgar Cayce readings say that Jesus' return will be in 1998.

5. The Last Jubilee Scroll says that the Melchizedek redivivus' return will be accompanied by a trumpet blast.

6. Jesus tells us that His return will be accompanied by a trumpet blast.

Most of the rest of this chapter is supportive of these points, which seem to be more than coincidental. Of course, all this may be just a coincidence (only time will tell for sure), but this timetable gives us something to look for in the coming years.

All the evidence we have looked at aside, no one can state for certain when the Second Coming will be. As the Bible says, "as to the day and the hour no man knoweth save the Father." This does not keep us from speculating, however, for we are curious creatures.

Symbolically that day will be a Day of Atonement, when the Man returns who was the sacrifice that "all could enter the holy of holies." It will be a time, as is written in Leviticus 25 and on the Liberty Bell, of "liberty throughout the land."

The Revelation

The Book of Revelation is a maze of symbols and archetypes that can be interpreted on both literal and symbolic levels. Much of the literal side of Revelation has been covered in our look at Old Testament prophecies, so in this chapter we will only deal with the symbolic interpretation.

"The Revelation" does not refer just to the Book of Revelation, but to a revelation which will sweep the entire world at the beginning of the New Age. This new awareness is what the Book of Revelation deals with, and so this will be our starting point. Edgar Cayce gave a series of readings on the Revelation in which he related its symbolism to the human body. It is this understanding of the human body which will be the breakthrough in coventional religious thought that will lead us into the New Age.

This new understanding involves the seven endocrine glands of the body, and is symbolized repeatedly in the Book of Revelation:

Chapter 1 - seven golden candlesticks, seven churches, seven angels
Chapter 4 - seven lamps, seven seals
Chapter 8 - seven angels
Chapter 13 - seven heads
Chapter 15 - seven plagues
Chapter 17 - seven heads, seven mountains

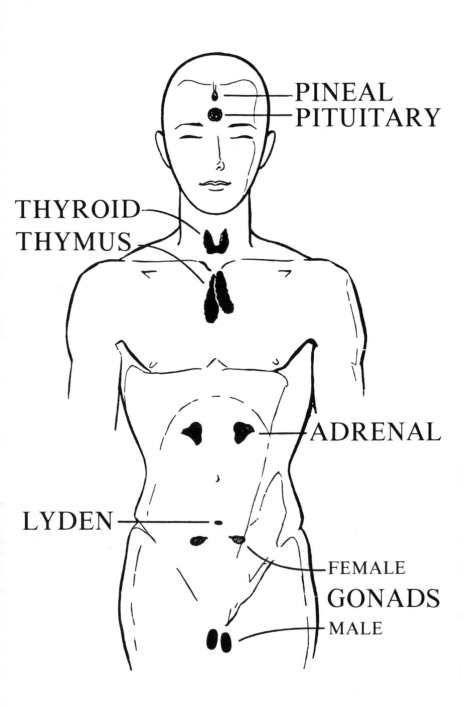

PINEAL
PITUITARY

THYROID
THYMUS

ADRENAL

LYDEN

FEMALE
GONADS
MALE

100

With all these "sevens" in Revelation it would seem that John's vision was trying to reveal something to us. The Cayce readings tell us that these "sevens" symbolically represent the seven endocrine centers of the human body.

These endocrine centers are known to the eastern religions as chakras. They are the pituitary, pineal, thyroid, thymus, adrenals, lyden, and the gonads. During meditation, energy known as kundalini is raised from the lyden and gonads through the nerve centers, up the spine to the brain, and finally to the pineal and pituitary glands. It is this upward flow of energy that allows a person to get in touch with his or her spiritual self. Cayce links these seven glands with the seven churches mentioned in the Book of Revelation and with the colors associated with each of the glands:

1. Pituitary - Violet, Laodicea - Highest Center
2. Pineal - Indigo, Philadelphia - Third Eye
3. Thyroid - Blue/Gray, Sardis - Will
4. Thymus - Green, Thyatira - Self-Gratification
5. Adrenals - Yellow, Pergamos - Self-Preservation
6. Lyden - Orange, Smyrna - Sustenance
7. Gonads - Red, Ephesus - Propagation of Species

The existence of these seven glands fits with what is known as the Law of Octaves. In music you move up seven notes before moving to a new octave: do, re, mi, fa, so, la, ti, do. The same is true of the endocrine system. We must move upward through this system in order to move out of what we call our physical universe.

The Law of Octaves is also demonstrated in nature by the fact that the genetic code, which transmits hereditary traits to offspring, contains 64 (8x8) bits of information. Man includes it in his own systems in the 64 elements of the I Ching, 64 squares on a chess board, and by the arrangement of all computers on a base 16 (2x8) system. So the Law of Octaves is present in all levels of nature.

Jesus said, "Destroy this temple and in three days I will raise it up." He was referring to the temple of the body, which He raised three days after His crucifixion. This is not the only human body symbolism in the Bible. In Revelation the beast rising out of the water symbolically represents the animal influences of the four lower centers: the thymus, adrenals, lyden, and gonads. In a similar vein, the sea of glass in Revelation 4:6 represents the calm emotions of John at the time of his vision. We meet the Father by calming our mind in meditation. This is symbolized by the sea of glass before the throne (the symbol for the brain). To complete the symbolism, in Chapter 5 the four and twenty elders represent the twenty-four cranial nerves of the brain's five senses.

Running between the seven endocrine centers and all the other centers in the body is the nerve system, referred to in the following section of Ecclesiastes as the "silver cord."

Ecclesiastes 12:5-7:

5   Also when they shall be afraid of that which is high, and fears shall be in the way, and the almond tree shall flourish, and the grasshopper shall be a burden, and the desire shall fail; because man goeth to his long home, and the mourners go about the streets;
6   Or ever the silver cord is loosed or the golden bowl is broken, or the pitcher is broken at the fountain, or the wheel broken at the cistern:
7   Then shall the dust return to the earth as it was, and the spirit shall return unto God, who gave it.

These verses are referring to the death of the body after the death of the nervous system. Electrical discharges produce a silver color (the silver cord), and the nervous system has a weak electrical current. So, this section of Ecclesiastes speaks of the human consciousness as contained within the nerve system. No doubt this is true, since everything we see, feel, smell, hear and taste is associated with the nerves of the body.

These nerves are also closely associated with the seven

endocrine centers. The seven glands affect the size of our bodies, our emotional and mental states, and just about everything else we are. Before we go any further it would be useful for us to examine each of these centers and their effects individually.

Gonads. The sexual center is the most basic center of all, since it is involved with the production of our physical bodies. Just as protons and electrons came together in the beginning to form hydrogen, the first element, so male and female come together to form our physical bodies. Thus, this center is linked to the production of matter. As we will see it is a very important point that the lower centers are linked to matter, and the higher centers are linked to energy. On the negative side the sex center provides lust, and on the positive side it provides opportunities for souls to enter the earth plane as newborn babies.

Lyden. There is not a great deal to be found in the way of information on the lyden. Cayce tells us it is involved with sustenance, or the absorption of food matter. It is the second point in the passage of energy through the system.

Adrenals. The adrenals are the glands of fear. They provide us with that sudden rush of tension when we are faced with danger. For their size the adrenals have a very large blood supply, so that their secretions can get into the system in a hurry. Meaner and more combative animals have a wide adrenal cortex while smaller, more timid animals have a narrow adrenal cortex. Man has the widest adrenal cortex of all. As a lower center, the adrenals produce fear hormones, fear being one of the most destructive emotions of all. It is no coincidence that fear is associated with a lower center while its opposite, faith, is associated with the higher centers.

Thymus. The thymus is called the gland of childhood because it is associated with our development at that stage. It stimulates the production of antibodies which protect the body from disease. The thymus is linked to the muscles and nutrition within our bodies. Cayce says that its emotion is love, and its location in the chest area may have something to do with the "heartache" we feel at times while in love.

Thyroid. The Cayce readings tell us that the thyroid is the gland of the will. This fits with what medical science tells us since the thyroid controls the amount of energy used in the body. Its hormone, thyroxin, controls energy output. If a person applies his will, he can always find enough energy to accomplish a task. The thyroid is the pivotal point between the four lower centers, and the two higher ones. The will controls which way the consciousness will go.

Pineal. Rene Descartes in his book, *Trait de L'Homme* in 1662, located the human soul in the pineal gland. 2,000 years ago the Hindus said the pineal was the "seat of the soul." Today, the pineal is often called the "third eye." This is fascinating since the cells in the pineal are almost identical to the cells in the retina of the eye. This may be why flashes of light are seen in higher states of consciousness. The mystical symbolism of the pineal is seen in the eye encased in the pyramid on the U.S. dollar bill. In the early days of science, dissected brains revealed lime salts in the pineal which were termed "brain sand." The pineal usually atrophies at age 7, which may be why Jesus said if we do not become "as little children" we cannot enter the kingdom of heaven. The pineal is the gateway to the highest center of all, the pituitary, since the pineal sits on the bundled nerves of the thalamus, from which the pituitary hangs.

Pituitary. The pituitary is called the master gland by doctors because it controls all the other glands. It is about the size of an almond dangling from the end of a group of nerves known as the hypothalamus. The pituitary is so important to the body that removal will cause death in three days. It has its own skull, known as the turkish saddle which cradles it within our larger skull. Sexual development is one of the pituitary's functions along with its more famous function of controlling the growth of the body. Underaction of the pituitary produces dwarfs, overaction produces giants.

Recent studies have shown that the pituitary produces natural painkillers known as endorphines. Western scientists have found that yogis trained in meditation can endure great physical pain by their production of endorphines. These endorphines may also be the cause of the "bliss" many people experience in meditation.

Last, but not least, the pituitary controls the salt content of the body. The salt content of any liquid is directly related to its electrical conductivity. It is possible that this would explain why healers, such as Jesus, could produce power to heal. Certainly this power also comes from higher levels, but at some point it must manifest itself on this level. Electrical impulses may be one of these manifestations.

These are only a few of the capabilities of the pituitary. Dozens of hormones that it produces have been isolated, many of which are unknown in their function. Ultimately, we will discover that the pituitary is unlimited in its functions. In meditation it is the point at which we enter the holy of holies within ourselves.

In light of our study of the two higher glands it is important at this point to examine the involvement of the brain during meditation. The human brain has been compared to a "delicate flower perched on the end of a slender stalk." There are three sections in the brain, called units. The third unit is concerned with planning and movement of the body. The second unit is concerned with the analysis of sensory input, e.g. seeing, hearing, etc. The first unit is the power supply. It is this unit that concerns us.

The *Encyclopedia of the Human Body* describes the first unit as follows:

The first unit
The first functional unit is located at the base of the brain and consists of the reticular formation, the midbrain, the thalamus and the hypothalamus. It is the first area encountered by inputs from the sense organs and information stemming from the metabolic functions within the body. This unit plays a role in the regulation of activity in the cortex and maintains the alertness of the higher areas of the brain. It does this

not by single isolated nerve impulses, but by waves of electrical activity spreading throughout the unit and traveling up to the cortex. It is similar to a power source, which feeds the higher areas and which, if removed, causes a state of drowsiness.

The pituitary and pineal are connected to the first unit at the hypothalamus and thalamus. During meditation the third unit of the brain is "shut off" by sitting still and not moving the body. The second unit is likewise shut off by clearing the mind of conscious thought. The only thing left is the first unit. As the quote indicates, waves of electrical energy flow up the spine to the thalamus, pineal, and the pituitary. This is the kundalini energy mentioned earlier. It is interesting to note that proper meditation requires calm emotions, and the thalamus when diseased, produces fits of strong emotion. So the flow of energy in the thalamus is linked to the emotions, the sea of glass, mentioned in Revelation by John.

All of this has been preached by mystics for thousands of years and is what Jesus meant when he said "the kingdom of God is within you."

The Cayce readings have a great deal to say about the kundalini as seen in the following readings:

Q-1. Are the following statements true or false? Comment on each as I read it: The life force rises directly from the Leydig gland through the Gonads, thence to Pineal, and then to the other centers.
A-1. This is correct: though, to be sure, as it rises and is distributed through the other centers it returns to the solar plexus area for its impluse through the system.

For the moment, let's consider the variation here in this life force — or as representing this life force. The question is asked not in relation to the life alone as manifested in the human body, but as to the process through which coordination is attained or gained in and through meditation, see?

Hence, physically, as we have indicated, there is first the nucleus — or the union of the first activities; and then the pineal as the long thread activity to the center of the brain, see? Then from there, as development progresses, there are those activities through reflexes to the growth or the developing of the body.

Interpret that variation, then, as being indicated here. One life force is the body growth, as just described. The other is the impluse that arises, from the life center, in meditation.

(281-53)

Q-1. How can I overcome the nerve strain I'm under at times?
A-1. By closing the eyes and meditating from within, so that there arises — through that of the nerve system —that necessary element that makes along the pineal (Don't forget that this runs from the toes to the crown of the head!), that will quiet the whole nerve forces, making for that — as has been given — as the true bread, the true strength of life itself. Quiet, meditation, for a half to a minute will bring strength — [if the body will] see physically this flowing out to quiet self, whether walking, standing still, or resting. Well, too, that oft, when alone meditate in the silence — as the body has done.

(311-4)

These readings show us that the flow of energy not only involves meditation, but body growth as well. This agrees with what medical science has told us. This flow of energy must be directed to spiritual things or it can be harmful. If used in the spirit of love and for the good of all, it can become a great Light as the following reading shows:

In the body we find that which connects the pineal, the pituitary, the lyden, may be truly called the silver cord, or the golden cup that may be filled with a closer walk with that which is the Creative Essence in physical, mental and spiritual life; for the destruction wholly of either will make for the disintegration of the soul from its house of clay. To be purely material minded, were an anatomical or pathological study made for a period of seven years (which is a cycle of change in all the body-elements) of one that is acted upon through the third eye alone, we will find one fed upon spiritual things becomes a light that may shine from and in the darkest corner. One fed upon the purely material will become a Frankenstein that is without a concept of any influence other than material or mental.

(262-20)

In this reading Cayce mentions the "silver cord," as written about in Ecclesiastes, which may be "filled with a closer walk with the Creative Essence" (God). It is interesting to note that Cayce says that one who acts through the third eye (pineal) alone for seven years (the period it takes for every cell in the body to replace itself) would become a "light to the world" while one fed only on the material world would become a Frankenstein monster! It is easy to think of examples of materially minded people in the world. (Frankenstein, if you will!). But it is encouraging to note that all of us can develop spiritually in just seven years if we so desire.

It may not be a coincidence that the Jewish sabbatical year comes every seven years. This may be to parallel the body change period. Even more significant, if the events of Daniel's seven year seventieth "week" are as easy to discern as we think, then everyone who becomes aware will have a final seven year period to develop themselves before the Second Coming. If people can be made aware of the starting point year of 1991, they can prepare themselves spiritually for 1998 by acting as Cayce says, "through the third eye alone." The clearly defined events of the seven year period will give everyone the chance to evolve to a higher level before the beginning of the millennium.

Development through meditation involves not only the act of meditation itself, but meditation with the highest possible purpose — in other words, being a channel of God's gifts to one's fellow man. What are these gifts? Love, patience, long-suffering, and forgiveness, to name just a few. With these purposes in mind meditation can become a most sublime and joyous experience.

I have been meditating for many years, so my experiences with meditation have been many, and varied. Many times I have received guidance from the "still small voice within." Usually this guidance has been of great help to me. The only bad experience I can remember involved an insect that insisted on buzzing around my ear during my meditation. This buzzing was such a disturbance, that the end of the meditation period found me exhausted from attempting to concentrate in an agitated frame of mind. The mind must be calm to properly meditate.

The rising of kundalini energy in meditation can be experienced in a variety of ways. It can be seen as a series of waves spreading outward from a single point, then dissipating and starting over again. It spreads like ripples in a pond when you toss in a rock. Or, to put it another way, it looks like water poured on flat concrete which spreads out in a circle from a single point. It slowly flows into one's consciousness.

Another kundalini experience is the bright light, or as some call it "seeing the light." It comes as a light brighter than any light ever seen with the eyes, except that it is in the mind's eye. Once, when I was falling asleep, I was viewing an extremely bright sunset. I was in a meditative state inside a totally dark room. I reacted to the sunset by trying to close my eyes, but found they were already closed! The "sunset" was inside my head. I have experienced this "light" several times since then, and it always occurs as an incredibly bright light between the eyes, the exact location of the pineal, the third eye.

The most vivid kundalini energy I have ever experienced happened to me in a recent meditation session. I had been reading about raising energy up the spine, and was attempting to do so just to see how much I could raise. This is not a good idea in any case because your purposes must be more pure than just having an "experience." Anyway, as I was raising this energy I visualized in my mind someone turning off a light. At the instant the light was turned off, I heard a loud audible snap! It sounded like a crackle of electricity or the snap of a bullwhip. At the same time I felt the energy flow going up my spine shut off with a sudden jolt. It was an unsettling experience that taught me that kundalini is not something to be toyed with.

As the Cayce readings have said, this electrical energy is not just for the growth of the body. The readings go even further: "Thus there are the vibrations of the electrical energies of the body, for Life itself is electrical..." (281-27)

About 50 years ago a Yale University neuroanatomist named Harold Burr found that there are electrical currents within all living organisms from seeds to human beings. He theorized that this electro-magnetic field doesn't just reflect the electrical activity of the cells it envelopes; it also controls and organizes them. Burr described it as "nature's jello mold," shaping living matter just as a magnetic field patterns iron filings.

Magnifying all this is the fact that the brain is the most electrical organ in the body. Neurons account for only 20 percent of the brain's cells, the rest are mostly glial cells, which sheathe the neurons. Evidence has been found that a direct current flows steadily through the glial cells. Some scientists now believe that this direct current system, generally ignored by most brain researchers, may be the body's natural mechanism for cellular growth and repair. Thus, science is gradually catching up with what the readings revealed many years ago.

This electrical current is very important to the theories we will look at next. The higher centers of the body are centers of energy, and the lower centers are more closely associated with matter.

The importance of this can be understood when one has a

grasp of Einstein's theory of relativity: As an object approaches the speed of light, time slows down. When said object reaches the speed of light, time stops. In other words, at the speed of light time does not move. This part of Einstein's theory was proven in 1936 by Bell Laboratories. A radiating atom can act as a clock because it emits light at a definite frequency and wavelength in precise intervals. This can be measured by a spectroscope. Bell Labs compared the light given off by hydrogen atoms at high velocities with that of hydrogen atoms at rest. It was discovered that the frequency of vibration of the fast-moving atoms slowed down in the exact manner Einstein had predicted. Another way of putting it would be that as the atoms speeded up, time slowed down.

Another example involves space travel. If a man left earth in a spaceship traveling at the speed of light, when he reached his destination he would be the same age as when he left. Even if several years had passed for people on the earth, our space traveler would not have aged at all. Even at the slow speeds automobiles and airplanes travel, time slows down, however slight the change may be. The change only becomes noticeable when speeds approach the speed of light, an incredible 186,000 miles a second.

All energy moves about the universe at the speed of light. So to energy and light, time is totally meaningless. Einstein put it as follows: "For us believing physicists time has the value of mere illusion, however tenacious." So time is an illusion belonging to the world of matter and not to the world of energy.

We know that consciousness operates through energy because the only thing that separates a dead body from a living body is electrical energy. The body without electricity is dead matter. At that point it exists only at the vibratory level of matter and not at the level from which our consciousness flows which is energy.

The train of logic is as follows: the direct current flow of electricity in the human brain moves at· 99.999% of the speed of light, in the wake of our consciousness. Our consciousness exists at the level from which light and energy come, where time is stopped. If our consciousness exists where time is standing still, then our consciousness is eternal. Our brain acts as a brake to slow our consciousness down enough that it can operate at a level where the illusion of time does exist, in our physical universe. This is the scientific proof that life is eternal. This is why the higher centers of the body are associated with energy, and the lower centers of the body are associated with matter.

If you raise your consciousness in meditation you connect with the energy level and your Eternal Being. Until recently this ramification of the theory of relativity has been ignored, but now many are beginning to look at the relationship between time, consciousness, and energy. Several books have been written on this subject and in the latter quarter of the 20th century discoveries in the world of physics will help awaken the world to the existence of eternal life.

The raising of consciousness to connect with the "eternal now" is the subject of the following Cayce reading:

> As this life-force is expanded, it moves first from the Leydig center through the adrenals, in what may be termed an upward trend, to the pineal and to the centers in control of the emotions — or reflexes through the nerve forces of the body.
>
> Thus an entity puts itself, through such an activity, into association or in conjunction with all it has EVER been or may be. For, it loosens the physical consciousness to the universal consciousness.
>
> (2475-1)4

Notice that Cayce says that moving upward to the pineal puts a person in contact with the past, present, and the future, the place where time does not move, and all time is one. This is the universal consciousness or God. Through this raising of energy we connect with God. This is nothing new. Mystics have been saying this for thousands of years, but now we know more about it through the realm of physics.

There are, of course, many connections between God and light energy. The sun, the source of all life and light, is the most obvious connection. Jesus emitted a light or aura which Matthew says was as "white as snow." Eastern mystics talk about achieving "enlightenment," with the middle syllable being the word "light."

The Bible is full of references to light. Some are references to spiritual light, but there is more in their meaning. Paul saw a great light on the road to Damascus that changed him from persecuting the Christians to joining them. Here are just a few biblical references to light:

John 1:5 "This then is the message which we have heard of Him and declare unto you, that God is light."

John 8:12 "I am the light of the world; he that followeth me shall not walk in darkness, but shall have the light of life."

John 12:36 "While ye have light, believe in the light, that ye may be the Sons of Light."

Matthew 6:22 "The light of the body is the eye."

Light is often used as a symbol of spirituality, even to the point of saying "God is Light." Jesus referred to Himself as the "light of the world" and to the light of the body as the "eye" or the third eye (pineal). Thus, Jesus has shown that the energy flow to the third eye is the spiritual light of the human body. This is the most important point in these references, because it shows the way of development for all of us.

In one of his readings, Cayce described the use of light appearing in a six-sided crystal as a "means of communication between the infinite and the finite." Since the source of light itself is the infinite, it would make sense that one could communicate with the "infinite" in this way. Just what this communication would mean we can only guess at this stage of our development.

One of the Cayce readings we looked at earlier referred to Jesus returning and receiving as many as had "quickened" themselves through living a spiritual life. All of the universe, matter and energy, is made up of vibrations. Energy is a quicker vibration than matter. The use of meditation and spiritual living quickens the body of matter to the level of energy, and beyond to the universal consciousness. "Quickening" is a perfect description of an increase in the frequency of vibrations, that is, a shift from matter to energy.

The raising of consciousness is central to the Second Coming: first because the raising of vibrations among the human race is what will attract Jesus to return; second because if one gets in touch with his or her eternal spirit, then physical death has no power. With all the earth changes that may occur, many people will die. But if they have quickened themselves, their spirits will live on and reincarnate during the millennium. So those who quicken themselves will "survive," even if they die.

Many books about the Second Coming speak of survival in terms of storing food and such, but true survival is based on the growth of a person's soul. This is clearly the message of Jesus' death and resurrection after three days in the tomb.

The length of Daniel's last week at seven years is a key point to this. Seven years is the length of time of the body's complete change period, during which every cell in the body is replaced. Everyone, as I have said before, will be given a chance to raise themselves and every cell in their bodies before He comes. There may even be what I will call an "endocrine judgement" when everyone is judged according to the level of energy involved with their seven centers. Certainly, we are all judged in this manner when we die, but during the changeover to the millennium this may happen to the living.

The idea of light and the raising of consciousness is relevant to the Second Coming for a number of other reasons. It represents the change that will occur in religious thought throughout the world. People will develop themselves through meditation, and science will come to recognize this development. Paticularly, the science of physics will lead the way in the field of understanding consciousness.

This understanding of consciousness includes much more than just the consciousness of man. Physics is moving toward understanding the universe and universal consciousness, an idea that has been held by Eastern religions for many years. The universe has been described as a thought in the mind of God, and now physicists are saying that the universe behaves more like "a great thought than a machine."

One of the most important theories developed in physics in the last few years is called Bell's theorem. In a series of very complicated mathematical proofs, physicist J.S. Bell has shown that everything in the universe is connected to everything else, even though they may be separated by great distances. Or in other words, everything is part of one thing, i.e., God, the Creative Force, etc.

There is evidence for this in other scientific truths. German physicist Max Planck proved that all energy radiations were a function of one number, now known, appropriately enough as "Planck's constant." If all energy is a function of one number, then surely all energy is a function of one thing. This one thing is the Creative Force or God.

Einstein proved that energy and matter were essentially equivalent, or were different vibratory levels of the same thing. Energy and matter are part of one force, or as the Bible says "The Lord, thy God is One."

This can be shown mathematically with Einstein's famous equivalence equation:

$$E = MC^2 \qquad \frac{E}{E} = \frac{MC^2}{E} \qquad 1 = \frac{MC^2}{E}$$

divide both sides by E

The information we have just looked at proves that the universe is a part of one whole. This whole is both physical and non-physical. Physical things exist in the third dimension, but the universe was created from the fourth dimension, the dimension of consciousness. Time is not the fourth dimension as many believe; thought, ideas, and consciousness are the fourth dimension. Before anything exists in the physical universe it must first be an idea. Before a bridge is built someone must think of the idea of building it. The same is true of the creation of the universe. God conceived of the universe first, and it was created. The point here is that the three-dimensional One we are part of is only part of the universal consciousness. Three dimensional reality is only a shadow of the spiritual reality. Everything in reality follows the same pattern: fourth dimensional idea $\longrightarrow$ creative action $\longrightarrow$ third-dimensional reality. This is the way our three-dimensional universe was created, and is still being created today.

In this chapter I have presented some of the changes in religious thought which will occur over the next few years. These changes in thought will contribute to the atmosphere before the Second Coming. New discoveries in physics will prove that the world is One which we call God.

Egyptian Prophecies

According to the Cayce readings, during the last part of this century, probably coinciding with the Second Coming, man will make an archeological discovery of profound significance. This discovery will involve the Egyptian pyramids at Gizeh. The Great Pyramid and the Sphinx, that mystery of mysteries, will yield treasures beyond the wildest dream of any Egyptologist.

The story of Gizeh goes back many thousands of years, before the Great Flood of Noah's time. During those ancient times, according to the readings, a king by the name of Arart moved his tribe into the Nile valley and conquered the natives there. Arart's spiritual leader was a priest by the name of Ra Ta, (a previous incarnation of Edgar Cayce). Inspired from on high, Ra Ta conceived a spiritual monument to last for all time, what is now known as the Great Pyramid at Gizeh. Hermes, who is often mentioned in Egyptian legends, was the architect of the project.

> ...the entering in of Hermes *with* Ra — who came as one of the peoples from the mount to which these peoples had been banished...Hence under the authority of Ra, and Hermes as the guide, or the actual (as would be termed in the present) constructing or construction architect with the Priest or Ra giving the directions.
>
> (294-151)

Arart's son, Araaraart, was king at the time of the completion of the project which is much older than generally believed.

Q-5. What was the date of the actual beginning and ending of the construction of the Great Pyramid?
A-5. Was one hundred years in construction. Begun and completed in the period of Araaraart's time, with Hermes and Ra.

Q-6. What was the date B.C. of that period?
A-6. 10,490 to 10,390 before the Prince entered into Egypt.

(5748-6)

The Great Pyramid was built by the use of forces we are only now beginning to rediscover.

Q-14. How was this particular Great Pyramid of Gizeh built?
A-14. By the use of those forces in nature as make for iron to swim. Stone floats in the air in the same manner. This will be discovered in '58.
(5748-6)

Q-3. By what power or powers were these early pyramids and temples constructed?
A-3. By the lifting forces of those gases that are being used gradually in the present civilization, and by the fine work or activities of those versed in that pertaining to the source from which all power comes.
(5750-1)

The force in nature that causes "iron to swim" is buoyancy. Buoyancy has been known since the time of Archimedes, but the method for focusing this force was not known until 1958 and still isn't totally understood. Many important discoveries were made in 1958 including the

118

invention of the laser. Since the readings say that the Atlanteans aided in the construction of the Pyramid, and since the readings also say that the principle source of power for the Atlantean civilization was light focused on a crystal, the laser may have been the method by which the forces of buoyancy were controlled.

> "For there was not only the adding to the monuments, but the Atlanteans aided in their activities with the creating of that called the Pyramid, with its records of events of the earth through its activity in all ages to that in which the new dispensation is to come."
>
> (281-43)

The Great Pyramid was constructed in a manner such that it would be difficult, if not impossible to reproduce it today. It contains 2,300,000 stones, many weighing as much as 20 tons. Its blocks are fitted together so finely that a razor blade cannot fit between the blocks. The technology used in its construction is superior to ours today because it was built by the Atlanteans.

According to the readings, the continent of Atlantis existed for thousands of years at a state of technology far beyond today's. But because of the misuse of this technology, the continent began to break up and sink into what is now the Atlantic Ocean. The total destruction took place over many years, and some Atlanteans escaped and found their way to Egypt and the Nile Valley.

Many Egyptologists would say that this story is pure fantasy, but several facts dispute this. The large pyramids in Egypt were allegedly tombs for ancient pharaohs, yet no bodies have ever been found in *any* of the larger pyramids. Grave robbers are always cited as the reason for this, but to reach the "King's Chamber" of the Great Pyramid, explorers had to dig around a 29-foot granite plug. When they reached the King's Chamber, it was empty. If grave robbers had been there before the exploration, would they have plugged the passage with a 29-foot thick granite stone to protect an empty tomb?

The Priest Ra and Hermes incorporated mathematics into the Pyramid including the relationship of pi and phi. This clearly shows that their knowledge of science was greater than that believed to be possessed by ancient man. These mathematical relations were not supposed to have been discovered until much later. (Many excellent books have been written on this subject, the best being Bill Fix's *Pyramid Odyssey*).

Geographical considerations also went into the building of the Great Pyramid.

"When the lines about the earth are considered from the mathematical precisions, it will be found that the center is nigh unto where the Great Pyramid, which was begun then, is still located."

(281-42)

"At the correct time accurate imaginary lines can be drawn from the opening of the Great Pyramid to the second star in the Great Dipper, called Polaris or the North Star. This indicates it is the system toward which the soul takes its flight after having completed its sojourn through this solar system."

(5748-6)

The Great Pyramid is arranged in a perfect north-south alignment, so close that after thousands of years it is off axis by only an inch or so. The entrance to the inner chambers is on an angle that faces directly toward Polaris, as mentioned in the previous reading. This indicates that each soul goes to that system after completing the cycle in this solar system. This is one of the more esoteric messages built into the Great Pyramid.

Much has been written in recent years of the special properties of the pyramid shape itself. Books about so-called "pyramid power" have testified to the ability of pyramids to do everything from sharpening razor blades to mummifying fruit. These effects are caused by the ability of the pyramid to focus cosmic energy. A pyramid can do this because it is a model of three dimensional reality. If you take a two-dimensional square, and use only one point to make it a three-dimensional object, the result is a pyramid. Thus, the Great Pyramid focuses cosmic energy by mirroring three-dimensional reality in on itself, in the same way that opposing mirrors make smaller and smaller images of each other into infinity.

The ability to focus energy is even contained in the name, "pyramid." "Pyra" comes from the word for fire, "pyro," and "mid" means middle. So, "pyramid" means "fire in the middle" or a focus of cosmic energy.

The Great Pyramid is built largely of limestone blocks which are made of small crystals. Limestone crystals are known for their even vibration and were chosen in order to focus the Pyramid's vibrations evenly. More will undoubtedly be learned about pyramid energy in the future as it is studied by modern-day science.

Not only is the Great Pyramid a focus of energy but it incorporates in its stones and inner passages, the history and future of man.

...the rise and fall of the nations were to be depicted in this same temple that was to act as an interpreter for that which had been, that which is, and that which is to be, in the material plane."

(294-151)

"This, then, receives all the records from the beginning of that given by the Priest, Arart, Araaraart and Ra, to that period when there is to be the change in the earth's position and the return of the Great Initiate to that and other lands for the folding up of those prophecies that are depicted there. All changes that came in the religious thought in the world are shown there, in the variations in which the passage through same is reached, from the base to the top — or to the open

121

tomb and the top. These are signified by both the layer and the color in what direction the turn is made."

(5748-5)

The rise and fall of nations are depicted in the Great Pyramid along with the changes in religious thought which will come about in the world. This can be seen by examining the passages. The first passage is descending, and this undoubtedly represents the fall of man from Grace. The next passage is ascending which represents man's ascent from the birth of Jesus to the present age. The stone prophecies continue until the return of the Great Initiate, Jesus, at the end of this age, 1998.

During Jesus' studies in Egypt, the Great Pyramid was used as a Hall of Initiation for Him and John the Baptist into the knowledge of One God.

"Then, with Hermes and Ra (those that assumed or took up the work of Araaraart) there began the building of that now called Gizeh, with which those prophecies that had been in the Temple of Records and the Temple Beautiful were builded, in the building of this that was to be the Hall of the Initiates of that sometimes referred to as the White Brotherhood."

(5748-5)

In this same Pyramid did the Great Initiate, the Master, take those last of the Brotherhood degrees with John, the forerunner of Him, at that place.

(5748-5)

This initiation involved breaking the cycle of death and rebirth, which Jesus did so dramatically with His Resurrection. The initiation in the Great Pyramid was a symbolic prelude to this.

Q-30. Please describe Jesus' initiation in Egypt, telling if the Gospel reference to "three days and nights in the grave or tomb," possibly in the shape of a cross, indicate a special initiation.

A-30. This is a portion of the initiation — it is a part of the passage through that to which each soul is to attain in its development, as has the world through each period of their incarnation in the earth. As is supposed, the record of the earth through the passage through the tomb, or the Pyramid, is that through which each entity, each soul, as an initiate must pass for the attaining to the releasing of same — as indicated by the empty tomb, which has never been filled, see? Only Jesus was able to break same, as it became that which indicated His fulfillment.

(2067-70)

Each soul in the earth plane must pass through the same sort of initiation in order to break the death cycle. Part of this initiation will be the darkness that will overcome the sun before the Second Coming. A more important part will be the recognition by everyone that death is not the end of life.

Of the prophecies represented in the Great Pyramid Cayce mentions several specifically.

Q-1. Are the deductions and conclusions arrived at by D. Davidson and H. Aldersmith in their book on The Great Pyramid correct?
A-1. Many of these that have been taken as deductions are correct. Many are far overdrawn. Only an initiate may understand.

Q-2. What corrections for the period of the 20th Century?
A-2. Only those that there will be an upheaval in '36.

Q-3. Do you mean there will be an upheaval in '36 as recorded in the Pyramid?
A-3. As recorded in the Pyramid, though this is set for

a correction which, as has been given, is between '32 and '38 — the correction would be, for this — as seen — is '36 — for it is in many — these run from specific days; for as has been seen, there are periods when even the hour, day, year, place, country, nation, town, and individuals are pointed out. That's how correct are many of those prophecies as made.

(5748-5)

According to the Cayce source, some of the prophecies in the Great Pyramid are correct down to the town, day, and individuals involved. What those prophecies could be, one can only guess, but no doubt that the birth of Jesus is one of the specific prophecies. Also there is mentioned an upheaval in 1936, estimated by the pyramid's prophecy in stone as occurring between 1932 and 1938. This upheaval is explained in the following readings:

A-1. A great deal in various experiences of same; that is, in the interpreting of periods of those activities which preceded that period in which the building was begun there. For, remember, this was not an interpretation only from that period but as to the very *place* and experience in which there is to be the change in the activities in the earth!

(849-45)

Q-4. What are the correct interpretations of the indications in the Great Pyramid regarding the time when the present depression will end?
A-4. The changes as indicated and outlined are for the latter part of the present year (1932). As far as depression is concerned, this is not — as in the minds of many — because fear has arisen, but rather that, when fear has arisen in the hearts of the created, sin lieth at the door. Then, the change will occur — or that seeking will make the definite change — in the latter portion of

the present year. Not that times financially will be better but the minds of the people will be fitted to the conditions better.

Q-10. What will be the type and extent of the upheaval in '36?
A-10. The wars, the upheavals in the interior of the earth, and the shifting of same by the differentiation in the axis as respecting the positions from the Polaris center.

(5748-6)

Two types of upheavals are discussed in this reading, wars and changes in the interior of the earth that will cause the poles to shift. 1936 was a turning point for World War II, since it was the year that Hitler became aggressive and marched into the Rhineland. Then, German armed forces were still weak, and if the Allies had resisted, Hitler's dominance of Europe might have been prevented. Also, 1936 was the beginning of the Spanish Civil War which became a mini-version of the larger war to come, with Fascism fighting democracy.

The upheaval within the earth which occurred in 1936 was apparently at the earth's core and will take time to work its way out. This is understandable since the earth is a revolving mass of molten nickel and iron, whose only solid portion is the thin layer of crust we live on. When a spinning top develops a slight wobble, it takes time to topple over, and the earth is no exception. A slight shift in equilibrium can gradually become a larger one.

Somehow the pole shift is represented in the stones of the Great Pyramid, and the following reading seems to imply that the constellation of Libra is involved.

(The Great Pyramid) was to be the presentation of that which had been gained by these peoples through the activities of Ra Ta, who now was known as Ra...(and) there was brought the idea of the preservation of these, not only for those in the present but for the generations that were to come in the experiences and experiences throughout that period, until the changes were to come again in the earth's position...It was formed according to that which had been worked out by Ra Ta in the mount as related to the position of the various stars, that acted in the place about which this particular solar system circles in its activity, going towards what? That same name as to which the Priest was banished — the constellation of Libra, or to Libya were these peoples sent.

(294-151)

It may be that the poles will shift toward Libra, or it may be that the whole solar system will shift. The reading is not clear. Cayce may have been referring to the earth and the moon as a "system." One thing that is known is that all the stars in the galaxy are constantly shifting position, and our sun and the pole star, Polaris, are no exceptions. Neither are the earth and the moon.

Of all the prophecies depicted in the Great Pyramid the most important has to do with the so-called "King's Chamber" at the top of the interior passageways. In the King's Chamber is an empty sarcophagus or coffin.

Q-7. What definite details are indicated as to what will happen after we enter the period of the King's Chamber?
A-7. When the bridegroom is at hand, all do rejoice. When we enter that understanding of being in the King's presence, with that of the mental seeking, the joy, the bouyancy, the new understanding, the new life, through the period.

Q-8. What is the significance of the empty sarcophagus?
A-8. That there will be no more death. Don't misunderstand or misinterpret! but the interpretation of death will be made plain.

Q-12. What is the date, as recorded by the Pyramid, of entering in the King's Chamber?
A-12. '38 to '58.

(5748-6)

The entity saw what was preserved as the memorials, the pyramids built during the entity's sojourn; when there was begun the Pyramid of understanding or Gizeh — and only to the King's Chamber was the pathway built. But the entity will see in the present the empty tomb period pass; hence rise to heights of activity in the present experience.

(275-33)

The meaning of the empty sarcophagus is that the death of the physical body does not mean the death of the soul. The prophecy connected with this is the return of the bridegroom, Jesus (as he is symbolized in the Bible), and the realization by the whole human race that the spirit survives death. This was the purpose of Jesus' resurrection, to allow a way for man to overcome death and to show that death could be overcome.

Above the empty sarcophagus in the King's Chamber are seven stones. These stones are arranged in the fashion of an arrow, with five stones as the shaft and two stones as the tip. This symbolizes the raising of energy through the seven endocrine centers. When you enter the King's Chamber you say, "Where has the body gone?" It has ascended upwards through the seven centers out of the physical plane. Remember that Cayce said that the King's Chamber represented the "changes that would occur in the religious thought of mankind." The most important change in religious thought will be the realization that the seven endocrine centers are the key to spiritual development. And the arrow points the way upward.

The five lower stones in the arrow are made of red granite, and represent the five lower centers of the body (thus the color red is used). The two stones at the top are

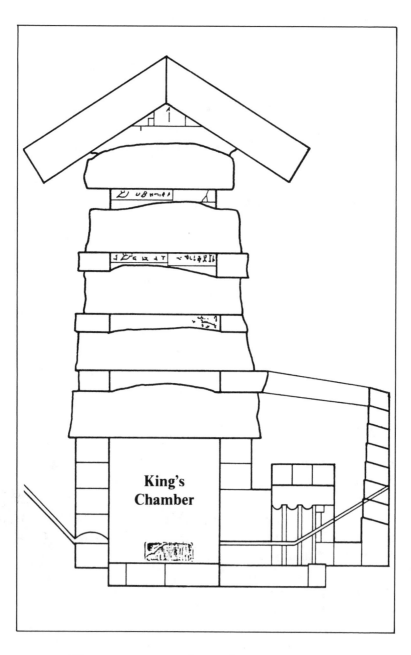

The seven stones above the King's Chamber.

made of gray limestone and represent the pineal and pituitary glands which are gray. The top two stones are connected, as the pituitary and pineal are connected by the thalamus and the hypothalamus. Even more esoteric is the fact that limestone was used. Lime accumulates in the brain such that years ago physicians called lime salts "brain sand." Also, the pituitary and pineal regulate the amount of lime in the body, so limestone was a perfect symbol for the two higher glands.

On the back of every U.S. dollar bill is a pyramid with an eye in the middle of it. The "eye in the pyramid" symbolizes the pineal or third eye of the body in beautifully mystical fashion. This eye also represents the seven stones above the empty sarcophagus, making one of the United States' most common symbols a very esoteric one.

Since the interior construction of the Pyramid is meant to relay prophecies about our time, it may be that the seven stones also have another meaning. We have already seen that the end of the age will be concluded by the seven year seventieth week of Daniel's prophecy. Therefore, the seven stones may symbolize the final seven year period before the Second Coming. This is implied in the previous reading by the fact that the date for the entering of the King's Chamber is '58 to '98. The prophecy for those forty years is contained in the empty sarcophagus and the seven stones topping it, so perhaps the seven year "week" is symbolized in the stones.

Next to the Great Pyramid of Gizeh is a monument the readings often call the mystery of mysteries, the Sphinx. Until recent times the Sphinx has been covered with sand up to its neck, but as the time has drawn near for the Sphinx to reveal its secrets, the whole body of the Sphinx has been uncovered. Its animal body represents man's animal nature, and the four lower centers of the body. The head of the Sphinx shows that the body of man is not just animalistic, but contains a spirit which can overcome his animal nature by developing the two higher centers contained in the head. The Sphinx symbolizes man's quest for spiritual development.

It is more than just a symbol, however, because for thousands of years the Sphinx has been guarding a storehouse of historical records known as the Hall of Records. This Hall of Records, buried beneath the sands of Gizeh, contains the history of man from the beginning including the rise and fall of Atlantis.

The entity aided in those activites, being among the children of the Law of One from Atlantis: *aiding* the Priest in that preparation, in that manner of building the temples of records that lie just beyond that enigma that still is the mystery of mysteries to those who seek to know what were the manners of thought of the ancient sons who made man — a beast — as a part of the consciousness.

(2402-2)

In the information as respecting the pyramids, their purpose in the experience of the peoples, in the period when there was the rebuilding of the Priest during the return in the land, some 10,500 before the coming of the Christ into the land, there was first that attempt to restore and add to that which had been begun on what is called the Sphinx, and the treasure or storehouse facing same, between this and the Nile, in which those records were kept by Arart and Araaraart in the period.

(5748-5)

These records, when they are found, will constitute the most incredible archeological find of all time. They contain not only the history of Atlantis but all of its spiritual truths that have been lost to man for thousands of years.

Q-4. In which pyramid or temple are the records mentioned in the readings given through this channel on Atlantis, in April 1932 (364 series)?

A-4. As given that temple was destroyed at the time there was the last destruction of Atlantis.

Yet, as time draws nigh when changes are to come

130

about, there may be the opening of those three places where the records are one, to those that are the initiates in the knowledge of the One God:

The temple by Iltar will then rise again. Also there will be the opening of the temple or Hall of Records in Egypt, and those records that were put into the heart of the Atlantean land may also be found there — that have been kept for those that are of that group.

The *records* are *One*.   (5750-1)

...these were to be kept as had been given by the priests in Atlantis or Poseidia (Temple), when these records of the race of the developments of the laws pertaining to One were put in their chambers...

(378-16)

The laws of One are the laws having to do with One God and were given by the priests in Atlantis to be preserved in the Hall of Records. However, there are two other places where the records are also preserved — in the temple of Iltar near the Yucatan in Mexico and underwater off the coast of what is now Bimini. These two locations were given in another reading. In those three places, "the records are one."

The records are not in any language with which we are familiar, but are written in a combination of Egyptian and Atlantean letters.

The entity was a priestess in the Law of One, and among those who — ill — came into the Egyptian land, as the elders in those groups for preserving the records, as well as for preserving a portion of that race, that peoples.

With the periods of reconstruction after the return of the Priest, the entity joined with those who were active in putting the records in forms that were partially of the old characters of the ancient or early Egyptian, part in the newer form of the Atlanteans.

These may be found, especially when the house or tomb of records is opened, in a few years from now.

(2537-1)

Q-2. Give in detail what the sealed room contains?
A-2. A record of Atlantis from the beginning of those periods when the Spirit took form or began the encasements in that land, and the developments of the peoples throughout their sojourn, with the records of the first destruction and the changes that took place in the land, with the record of the sojournings of the peoples to the varied activities in other lands, and a record of the meetings of all the nations or lands for the activities in the destructions that became necessary with the final destruction of Atlantis and the buildings of the Pyramid of Initiation, with who, what, where, would come the opening of the records that are as copies from the sunken Atlantis; for with the change it must rise (the temple) again.

This in position lies, as the sun rises from the waters, the line of the shadow (or light) falls between the paws of the Sphinx that was later set as the sentinel or guard, and which may not be entered from the connecting chambers from the Sphinx's paw (right paw) until the time has been fulfilled when the changes must be active in this sphere of man's experience.

Between, then, the Sphinx and the river.

(378-16)

According to Cayce the records also contain a prophecy of who will find them, when this will happen, and where they will be found. The connecting chambers will be opened from the Sphinx's right paw, and this gives us a tremendous clue as to where the entrance to the Hall of Records is. Of course, people familiar with the readings have examined the Sphinx's right paw for years and the entrance has not yet been found, but there may be a helpful clue in the following reading:

Q-2. In what capacity did this entity act regarding the building of the Sphinx?

A-2. As the monuments were being rebuilt in the plains of that now called the pyramid of Gizeh, this entity builded, laid the foundations; that is, superintended same, figured out the geometrical position of same in relation to those buildings as were put up of that connecting the Sphinx. And the data concerning same may be found in the vaults in the base of the Sphinx. We see this Sphinx was builded as this:

The excavations were made for same in the plains above where the temple of Isis had stood during the deluge, occurring some centuries before, when this people (and this entity among them) came in from the north country and took possession of the rule of this country, setting up the first dynasty. The entity was with that dynasty, also in the second dynasty of Araaraart, when those buildings were begun. The base of the Sphinx was laid out in channels, and in the corner facing the Gizeh may be found the wording of how this was founded, giving the history of the first invading ruler and the ascension of Araaraart to that position.

(195-14)

This reading tells us that at the corner base of the Sphinx facing Gizeh (the Great Pyramid) is the wording of how the Sphinx was founded and the history of Arart and his son Araaraart. On this corner of the Sphinx is a small rectangle about ten feet high which I call a "box." Located on the other side of the Sphinx near the right forepaw is another identical box.

One of these boxes of stone is by the corner facing the Great Pyramid, where records are located according to Cayce, and the other box is by the right forepaw where the entrance to the Hall of Records is located. It may be a coincidence, but these boxes are located right where Cayce says there are underground chambers. Also significant is

The Sphinx's right front forepaw "box".

(Photo by Uwe E. Wilken)

that no mention is made in any of the hieroglyphs concerning these boxes. Why? Perhaps they were to remain a secret until the time was ripe.

In the 1920s when the Sphinx was dug out of the sand, a statue of the Egyptian god of the underworld was found in pieces on top of the box by the right forepaw. Legend has it that a Pharaoh dismantled the box and discovered an underground passage leading from it. When his men went into the passage, they came out covered with painful sores. So the Pharaoh had the box sealed and a statue of the god of the underworld placed on top of it. If this legend is true the Pharaoh's men may have discovered the entrance to the Hall of Records, and then sealed it back up.

In 1982 S.R.I., Inc. (formerly Stanford Research Institute) did acoustical soundings underneath the right front paw of the Sphinx, and what they found is very interesting. Under the entire length of the right paw they got a good clear signal which indicates that there are no underground passages there. But directly under the right front paw box the signal was dead in three places, as though some kind of opening or empty space was blocking the signal. These dead spots may be the passageway that the Pharaoh's men found.

When Cayce was alive, he did a series of readings for a man he said would be one of the ones to rediscover the Hall of Records. During the building of the Great Pyramid this man lived in Egypt, and his name at that time was Hept Supht. According to Cayce, Hept Supht means "keep it shut." He was in charge of closing up the records and keeping them shut until the time was right. He asked Cayce the following question:

Q-4. Am I the one to receive directions as to where the sealed room is and how to find it?
A-4. One of the two. Two with a guide. Hept-Supht, El-ka, and Atlan. These will appear.

(378-16)

Since the man asking the question died in 1960, it is apparent that he will make the discovery during a more recent incarnation, one that probably began in the last few years. Two others will appear to join him, Atlan and El-ka by their Atlantean names. Hept Supht will find the records because he was the one that sealed them thousands of years ago during an elaborate ceremony.

And, as this was to be (Gizeh we are speaking of) the place for the initiates and their gaining by personal application, and by the journey or journeys *through* the various activities — as in the ceremonial actions of those that became initiates, it became very fitting (to those as in Ra, and those of Ra-Ta) that there should be the crowning or placing of this symbol of the record, and of the initiates' place of activity, by one who represented both the old and the new; one representing then the Sons of the Law in Atlantis, Lemuria, Oz and Og. So, he that keeps the record, that keeps shut, or Hept-Supht, was made or chosen as the one to *seal* that in the tomb.

The ceremony was long; the clanging of the apex by the gavel that was used in the sounding of the placing. Hence there has arisen from this ceremony many of those things that may be seen in the present; as the call to prayer, the church bell in the present, may be termed a descendant; the sounding of the trumpet as the call to arms, or that as revelry; the sound as of those that make for mourning, in the putting away of the body; the sounding as of ringing in the new year, the sounding as of the coming of the bridegroom; *all* have their inception from the sound that was made that kept the earth's record of the earth's building, as to that from the change. The old record in Gizeh is from that as recorded from the journey to Pyrenees; and to 1998 from the death of the Son of Man (as a man).

(378-14)

The following readings talk about when the records will be found:

As for the physical records — it will be necessary to wait until the full time has come for the breaking up of much that has been in the nature of selfish motives in the world. For, remember, these records were made from the angle of *world* movements. So must thy activities be in the present of the universal approach, but as applied to the individual.

(2329-3)

For, as known to all God IS! And the soul that becomes more and more aware of His, God's use of Man, that all may know of His Presence, is becoming then in atonement; as self was in the experience, and preserved that record for the future entering souls, that will be physically known when time has set its mark.

(378-16)

This may not be entered without an understanding, for those that were left as guards may *not* be passed until after a period of their regeneration in the Mount, or the fifth root race begins.

(5748-6—

The records will not be found until there is the "breaking up of selfish motives in the world," and "time has set its mark." Clearly the selfish motives of the world will not be broken up until 1998, and so the opening of the Hall of Records will probably coincide with the Second Coming. Man could not handle the technological advances contained in the records without a spiritual understanding.

Cayce links the discovery of the records with the beginning of the "fifth root race" and according to the writings of Madam Blavatasky the fifth root race, or the change of man to a more spiritual self, will not begin until Jesus returns. So this is more evidence that the Hall of Records will not be opened until 1998.

Jesus said, "I will bring all things to thine remembrance." This was not only a reference to remembrance of past lives, but to the revelation of man's whole history with the Second Coming. There will be no more debate between creationist and evolutionist. The true story of man's creation and destiny will be known to *all*.

We have so much to look forward to during the next few years, the Second Coming of Jesus and the opening of the Hall of Records with all of man's rich history. It will be a wonderful beginning to the New Age.

The Hopi

The Hopi Indians of the American Southwest have a long, deep and spiritual history. The Hopi live on the Black Mesa of Northeastern Arizona, an area of land which rises thousands of feet above the surrounding plain. They live a simple way of life, farming and maintaining the rhythm of life that has been theirs for thousands of years. They have never been to war with the white man preferring to remain a separate entity. This nature is reflected in their name, Hopi, which means "peaceful people."

The Hopi's story of creation is almost identical to our own. In the beginning the Taiowa (the Infinite) created the Sotuknang (the Finite); and God (the Infinite) created the heavens and the earth (the Finite). Taiowa ordered Sotuknang to create the twins, Poquanghoya and Palongawhoya. Poquanghoya and Palongawhoya were sent to the north and south poles to keep the earth turning. This legend of a positive and negative force corresponds with what scientists tell us was the first element, hydrogen, which is made of one positive particle (proton), and one negative particle (electron).

The Hopi have a history of several worlds preceding the present one, each destroyed by calamity. These worlds were destroyed by the same things that many other sources tell us were the methods of destruction in our own history: fire, ice and flood. According to the Hopi, during the first world, life was in harmony with the infinite. People gradually fell out of harmony with the infinite, however, and according to the *Bear Tribe's Self Reliance Book* (which recounts Hopi history) man "lost the use of the vibratory center on the top of the head (kopave), and the soft spot that was the doorway between the body and the spirit hardened." This fits with what we know about the pituitary gland, the psychic center in the brain where we can attune to the infinite. The Hopi thus recorded what we know as the Fall from Grace in their legends.

The Hopi record that God destroyed the first world by fire.

"Taiowa decided that would never do, and so he ordered Sotuknang to destroy the world, but to save a few people from destruction. He led them into the center of the world, where they were received by the Ant People. The Ant People fed them so well that they, themselves, began to grow thin. (It is said that this is the reason why today the Ant People have such thin waists.) As the people stayed underground, the volcanoes on the surface of the First World erupted, and the whole world caught fire. After the fires subsided, the people came up from their shelter and began to move to the Second World that had been prepared for them."

The Second World was destroyed by ice.

"Here, again, the people lived until they forgot their origin and grew cold and hard to the ways of the Good Life. And so, once again, Sotuknang was ordered to destroy the world. This time he ordered the Twins, Poquanghoya and Palongawhoya, to leave their stations at the North and South Poles and let the world be destroyed. They did this, after the people had again hidden with the Ant People underground. After the Twins left their stations, the world's stability was removed and so it flipped end over end and everything on it was destroyed by ice."

This legend of a pole shift and an ice age agrees with what we have learned about the last pole shift which occurred approximately 45,000-48,000 B.C.

The world before the present one was, according to the Hopi, destroyed by the flood. This corresponds to all the legends and history of the so-called "Great Flood." The story of Noah and his ark is the one most of us are familiar with in this regard. Taiowa destroyed the last world by sending high waves over the continents. This fits with the description in the Cayce readings of the destruction of Atlantis, an event that preceded the present era. Of course, the sinking of the continent of Atlantis is recorded in other sources as well, including Plato. All this brings us to the fourth world of today.

What interests us about the Hopi's view of the Fourth World is its future. The Hopi tradition includes prophecies just like the white man's. The culmination of these prophecies will be "Purification Day" when evil will be eliminated and peace will rule the land. Several events were predicted by the Hopi leading up to Purification Day. Wagons linked together and pulled by something other than a horse was one of the first signs predicted. This was fulfilled by the white man's railroad. Cobwebs in the air, roads in the sky, and lines across the land were also predicted. Airline routes and highways fulfilled these prophecies.

A "gourd full of ashes" would be invented, according to the Hopi, which would cause destruction, boiling rivers and burning land. The Hopi believe the explosion of the Hiroshima atomic bomb fulfilled this prophecy.

One of the last signs will be when the white man puts his "house in the sky." After that, great changes will be in store for the people of the earth. Man's meddling with the forces of nature will cause the earth and its people to be out of balance, causing great destruction. The Hopi believe that the United States space station Skylab was the "house in the sky" of their prophecy. Skylab was launched in the mid-1970s.

The religious leaders of the Hopi tribe, the spiritual elders, decided in 1948 that the prophecies were beginning to come true, and they should act. First, they decided to reveal to the world the prophecies of their people. One part

141

of these prophecies foretold of a great "house of mica" standing on the eastern shore of America that would be a place where the leaders of the world would assemble. Mica is very similar to glass, and the Hopi interpreted this to be a reference to the United Nations building in New York City. The Hopi were to go to the house of mica three times, and if they were rejected, then they were to return to their home and await the Day of Purification.

Twice the Hopi went to the General Assembly, in 1948 and 1973, and both times they were not allowed to speak. In 1976 after two attempts, the Hopi were allowed to speak at a U.N. sponsored Habitat Conference in Vancouver. Their speaker was Thomas Banyacya, their religious leader. Part of his speech follows:

"The message today is our third and perhaps final attempt to inform the world of the present status of Man's existence on our Earth Mother. We are not asking the United Nations for help in any material way. We are, according to Hopi prophecy, simply trying to inform the world of what is going to happen if the destruction of the earth and its original peoples continues as is known by our religious Hopi elders. We do not come before the United Nations in order to join it. We come to fulfill Hopi sacred mission and ancient prophecy in order to find one, two or three nations who should now recognize their sacred duty to stop the destruction of the First People's land and life throughout the western hemisphere. We, Hopi, know that there are one, two or three nations here in the United Nations that could listen to our message and understand it so that they can fulfill their mission, and whatever results from your failure to fulfill your sacred responsibilities to stop all of this destruction, genocide, harassment, imprisonment, oppression and lack of respect for Native Brothers will be of your own doing because we, the First Peoples of the western hemisphere, have carried out our sacred duty by bringing this spiritual message of warnings and hope for the future to your attention."

One of the keys to the Hopi prophecy is their interpretation of a petroglyph that is carved on rock in the middle of the Hopi Black Mesa.

The knowledge of world events has been handed down in secret religious societies of the Hopi. The leaders throughout each generation have especially watched for a series of three world-shaking events, each accompanied by a particular symbol. These symbols — the swastika, the sun and the color red — are inscribed upon a rock and on the sacred gourd rattle used in Hopi ceremonies. From the sacred teachings the Hopi knew that out of the violence and destruction of each world-shaking and purifying experience, the strongest elements would emerge with a greater force to produce the next event. (World War II championed by Germany and its swastika, merged later with Japan, "Land of the rising sun.") When these symbols appeared on the international scene, it was very clear to the Hopi that a major and final phase of world prophecy was being fulfilled and they then released for humanity (in 1948) many of the secret teachings in order to help offset the third and final 'great purification' which on the petroglyph is portrayed by a red hat and cloak. According to the Hopi elders, 'The red hat and cloak people will have a huge population.' They will invade this land in a single day 'like a swarm of locusts' and the sky will be darkened with them as they come. This prophecy is similar to the biblical Revelation which speaks of the great Red Dragon which threatens nations and the invasion by 'the Kings of the East' and 200 million horsemen.

As we can see, the Hopi prophecy fits Revelation's description of an invasion by a massive army, possibly the Chinese. The red hat and cloak fit this imagery since the symbol of the Chinese is the communist red flag. In addition, the Chinese army has a red insignia on their uniforms. The Hopi prediction that the sky will be darkened during this time agrees with the Bible's prediction. All of this is associated with a Day of Purification paralleling the "Judgment Day" of the Bible.

The Purification Day will bring the return of the "True White Brother," according to the Hopi. The True White

143

Brother will be one of the people who will cause the Purification Day to occur. The story of this "True White Brother" is as follows:

After the destruction of the Third World by Flood, the Great Spirit created a set of stone tablets which contained all the teachings, prophecies, and warnings necessary for the safety of the Fourth World. These stone tablets were given to the Hopi chief that led the tribe into their present home, after the destruction of the Third World. The stone tablets were to provide the information for maintaining the harmony and balance of the new world.

The chief left the tablets to his two sons when he died, dividing them between the two. The older brother took one of the tablets East. After reaching the East he was to return and look for his younger brother and together they were to bring about the Purification Day, so that evil could be eliminated from the earth, and harmony return. The brothers would know each other because they would have matching stone tablets. The younger brother would recognize his older brother because he would have a lighter complexion, a true white brother (thus the name), and would be wearing a red cap or a red cloak. This is the myth the Hopi have retained of the True White Brother.

Of course, our point of view is that the True White Brother is Jesus and that the Purification Day is what we call Judgment Day. All of this once again fits the Bible's view. Even more interesting is the reference to stone tablets which detail a plan for harmony and balance. Could this be the Hall of Records in Egypt? They contain teachings and prophecies just like the ones described in the Hopi prophecy. The Egyptian records were made and put away just after the destruction of the Third World, another parallel to the prophecies of the Hopi. The legend of the stone tablets may be a historical account of the Hall of Records passed down through generations and generations of Hopi.

The *Mexico Mystique* by Frank Waters tells us more about the Day of Purification.

"As the Day of Purification approaches, the True White

Brother will come. He will bring with him sacred stone tablets to match those given the Hopis long ago. With him will come two helpers. One will carry the swastika, male symbol of purity, and a cross, female symbol of purity. The second helper will carry the symbol of the sun. These two will shake the earth. There will be a massive explosion, perhaps a volcanic eruption that will be felt throughout North and South America."

"If these three fulfill their mission, finding a few Hopis who steadfastly adhere to their ancient teachings, they will lay out a new life plan. The earth will become new as it was in the beginning. The people saved will share everything in common, speak one tongue, and adopt the religion of the Great Spirit, Massau. But if the three sacred beings fail in their mission, and all people still remain corrupt, the Great Spirit will send "One" from the West. He will be many, many people and unmerciful. He will destroy the earth, only the ants being left to inhabit it."

This passage parallels the earth changes predicted in the Bible. The concept of the millennium is described by the Hopi as the world adopting the religion of the Great Spirit, and sharing resources in common.

Tom Tarbet in an article entitled "The Essence of Hopi Prophecy" from the *East West Journal* (October 1977) tells us more:

"The final stage, called the "great day of purification," has also been described as a "mystery egg," in which the forces of the swastika and the sun, plus a third force, symbolized by the color red, culminate in either total rebirth or total annihilation — we don't yet know which, but the choice is ours. War and natural catastrophe may be involved, the degree of violence determined by the degree of inequity among the peoples of the world, and the amount of imbalance in nature. In this crisis, rich and poor will be forced to struggle as equals to survive."

"That it will be very violent is now almost taken for granted among traditional Hopi, but humans may still lessen the violence by correcting their treatment of nature and fellow humans. Ancient spiritually based communities, such as the Hopi, must especially be preserved and not forced to abandon their wise way of life and the natural resources they have vowed to protect."

The Hopi believe, as do many others, that the degree of violence associated with the coming changes is dependent upon how well humanity is in harmony with the earth and the Great Spirit, God. If there is equality among the nations and people of the world, then the changes will be less severe. If we upset the "balance of nature" by our actions with respect to the earth, then the earth will react violently. This we have discussed before.

The Hopi prophecies agree with the other prophecies we have looked at in several different categories.

1. There will be a Purification Day when wickedness will be destroyed (Judgment Day).
2. There will be an invasion by a country with a large population (army of 200 million in Revelation).
3. The sky will be darkened.
4. Tablets will be revealed containing ancient teachings (Egyptian Hall of Records).
5. A True White Brother will return on Purification Day (Jesus' return).
6. Earth changes will accompany this Day of Purification.
7. The world will live in harmony and adopt one religion (the millennium).

All in all the Hopi prophecies parallel the Bible remarkably, hitting almost all the same key points. It shows that religions of different cultures can arrive at the same conclusions from different paths. These prophecies also make the Bible seem even more amazing, since most of its prophets made these same predictions 2,000 or more years ago.

The Hopi through time have shown themselves to be a spiritual people. The accuracy of their prophecies confirms this. Hopefully, the world will listen to their warning and prepare in harmony before the Day of Purification comes.

The Millennium

As time goes by we need to give more and more thought about our own attitude toward the Second Coming. The great tribulation and the changes in the earth are merely the birth pains of a new age, something which is unpleasant, but which must be experienced if this new "baby" is to be born. We should not look on the changes with fear, even though it is hard not to sometimes. As Richard Bach wrote in his book *Illusions*, "What the caterpillar calls the end of the world, the master calls a butterfly." It all depends on your point of view when you look at it.

The Second Coming itself will, I am sure, be totally different than we think it will be. It will be more dynamic and beautiful and will affect more people than we can imagine. The entire world will undergo a tremendous transformation, a revolutionary change on all levels. People will feel the urgency of this change as we approach the end of this century. They will feel a sense of His presence, both in a physical sense with His appearance and in the individual sense within their own hearts. For it is within our hearts that we meet Him.

When Jesus appears, He will be loving and forgiving. He will embody all the positive characteristics a human being can have. He will be as wonderful as we expect Him to be, and more... God's love flowing through one Man.

His mere physical appearance is not the extent of the change, however, for He stood in people's presence 2,000 years ago,, and it did not change their hard hearts. Thus, the change must be within us, and as such we all have a part in the Second Coming. This is a great opportunity for all of us, for we can be a part of the most joyous change in the history of man. No one will be kept from participating if he or she wants to.

We need to prepare ourselves mentally and spiritually for this new day. First through the desire to be a part of it, and then through actions to make it come about in a more positive fashion. If in our day-to-day living we reflect His love, we will be contributing positively to the atmosphere of expectancy. If we can be a little kinder, a little more forgiving we will be contributing to the change. This is surely what is needed in the world today.

In the way of physical preparations, these need to be made, but this has been overemphasized by many people. It is said that we should head for the countryside, build fortresses, store food, and prepare for the end. The term "survivalists" has been coined by the press to describe people who preach this type of preparation. Even though storing food may be a good idea, in general the "survivalist" attitude isn't the best attitude to take. John White, author of *Pole Shift,* tells a story about a group of survivalists in Oregon. They bought land in the country, build underground bunkers, stored food, brought in their yogurt makers, and Browning automatic rifles to prepare themselves for the disintegration of society at the end of the age. A year after the group formed, the leader died of a heart attack. The doctors said it was stress related! Obviously, he took the wrong attitude toward the coming changes seeing them as confrontational. Our mental and spiritual preparation is more important than the physical. No amount of physical preparation is going to save you if you are not ready spiritually.

The millennium itself is something to be looked forward to with great joy. Political, economic, and social institutions will be set up on a much more equitable basis than they are today. No wars, strife, civil disorder, oppression, or denial of people's rights will be tolerated. Jesus will rule the nations with a "rod of iron." No more will the nations of the world waste 800 billion dollars a year on weapons of destruction as they do today. Those resources will go to the improvement of life for every individual soul on the earth, not for the glory and power of a few at the top.

A new brand of science will emerge based on the understanding of the One Force in the universe. This science will extend life expectancy far beyond what it is today. People will live a long, long time (as we are told they did in Biblical times). Some may live as long as Methuselah who, according to the Bible, lived to be over 900 years old.

The purpose of the millennium will not be just to snatch a few souls up to heaven leaving the rest behind. Rather, the purpose of the millennium is to continue the work of saving souls from separation from God. The greatest sin is to be separated from God, or to be unaware of His presence, and a soul can only will this on itself. For as has been said, "God has not willed that any soul should perish but has prepared for each a way of escape." An all-knowing, all-loving God would not want for any to perish, not *one*. So during the millennium and after, the work of soul attunement will go on. No souls will be lost unless they will it.

All that is necessary for us to be a part of the millennium is a desire to be there, and the willingness to align our wills with God's Will. Here's hoping that all who read this will experience the great joy that lies ahead.

Revelation 7:14-17

14   These are they who came out of the great tribulation, and have washed their robes, and made them white in the blood of the Lamb.

15   Therefore are they before the throne of God, and serve him day and night in his temple; and he that sitteth on the throne shall dwell among them.

16   They shall hunger no more, neither thirst any more; neither shall the sun light on them, nor any heat.

17   For the Lamb who is in the midst of the throne shall feed them, and shall lead them unto living fountains of waters; and God shall wipe away all tears from their eyes.